A TREMOR
of BLISS

A TREMOR *of* BLISS

Sex, Catholicism, and Rock 'n' Roll

MARK JUDGE

IMAGE • NEW YORK

Published in the United States by Doubleday Religion, an imprint of the
Crown Publishing Group, a division of Random House, Inc., New York.
www.crownpublishing.com

IMAGE, the Image colophon, and DOUBLEDAY are registered trademarks
of Random House, Inc.

Library of Congress Cataloging-in-Publication Data

Judge, Mark Gauvreau, 1964–
A tremor of bliss: sex, Catholicism, and rock 'n' roll/Mark Judge.—1st ed.
p. cm.
Includes bibliographical references and index.
1. Sex—Religious aspects—Catholic Church. 2. Catholic
Church—Doctrines. I. Title.
BX1795. S48J83 2010
233'.5—dc22
2010009036

ISBN 978-0-385-51920-5

Printed in the United States of America

Design by Lauren Dong

1 3 5 7 9 10 8 6 4 2

First Edition

For Tejal

Contents

Introduction 11

Chapter One
MY FOOLISH HEART 25

Chapter Two
YEAR ZERO 47

Chapter Three
PHENOMENOLOGY 77

Chapter Four
THE NEW COMSTOCKERY 107

Chapter Five
ASTRAL WEEKS 149

Acknowledgments 185
Bibliography 187

I have had a tremor of bliss, a wink of heaven,
    a whisper,
And I would no longer be denied; all things
Proceed to joyful consummation.

—T. S. ELIOT

I can't help thinking we grew up too fast.

—THE MORNING BENDERS

Introduction

THIS BOOK BEGAN AS A CHAPTER I DIDN'T WANT to write. In 2006 I had been contracted to write a book about Catholicism; the theme was how liberal and conservative Catholics could end the disputes that have divided them for forty years. I had hoped to lay out ten basic things, from abortion to the liturgy, that both sides could agree on. Where the liberals would at long last concede that abortion was a unique evil that could not be defended, conservatives might be convinced that laws that attempt to deport up to ten million illegal immigrants and send them back home, despite how poor and desperate they are, are unjust. My book was about how both sides of the Catholic culture war could achieve peace by—well, by following the teachings of the Church.

The first chapter in the book was going to be about

sex. I wanted to write about sex first not because I found it the most interesting, but because I wanted to get it out of the way. I still had a reticence about sex that went back to the way I was raised, by parents who were by no means prudes, but who also never talked about sex. I also am a sinner and a faulty vessel and wanted to avoid sounding like a conservative scold about sexual matters. So the first chapter would be about sex and then I could go on to less chaotic and terrifying topics.

But then something happened. While doing research, I came across some of the most poetic, beautiful, inspiring writing about human sexuality—and it was all written or said by Catholics. Much of it came from the years before Vatican II, the Church council from the early 1960s that supposedly modernized the Church. I had thought that before the council the world, and especially the Catholic Church, was lost in a puritanical darkness that dared not speak of the human body. Then I came across writers like Saint Teresa of Avila, who lived in the sixteenth century and used erotic metaphors to describe our seduction by God, and the genius Dietrich von Hildebrand, who spoke openly about the power of the orgasm—in 1925. Then there was Pope John Paul II and his *The Theology of the Body*. In *The Theology of the Body*, John Paul II goes back to Genesis to reveal the true meaning of love and the human body. In it, John Paul II emphasizes that man— meaning persons—were made in the image of God.

When we are seeing another person, we are seeing the image of God. And we become even more like God through the act of loving that person—as a person, in the image of God, not as a thing. And we can come to know mastery of ourselves and our sexuality by realizing that we ourselves are also created in the image of God. When we come to know this fully, we can come to realize genuine freedom. John Paul II talks about the Song of Songs, those wonderful, and even steamy, love poems of the Old Testament, not as a metaphor of the love of God for His people, as was traditionally done in Catholicism, but as the reflection of a very real event— the love of Adam and Eve before the Fall. In one crucial passage, John Paul II contradicts the notion that God made Eve as a "helper" so she could get next to Adam to push the plow in the Garden of Eden. In fact, Eve's help was spiritual help. She would do no less than make it possible for Adam to experience the Trinitarian love of God. Prior to this, Adam "sensed that he was alone." He was different from the animals, and while in communion with God, he was not God. Eve, rather than bringing about Adam's ruin, allowed him to experience the interior life of God.

For the past fifty years—indeed the last one hundred years—a crusade has been fought to defuse the basic reality of sex as a unique, supernatural experience of its power. We have shaken off the sexual reticence of our parents and grandparents, which was often unhealthy, and replaced it with an unimaginative frankness—human sexuality as plumbing. Television, movies, journalists, and teachers have slowly stripped sex of its mystery and power, ironically in the name of greater freedom and understanding. To them, sex will become healthy and free once it is accepted that the human body and the conjugal act are nothing to get excited about. Humans need to have sex for health and well-being—in this regard we are not that different from animals. To many pop stars with limited talent, sex is a way to gain legitimacy with those in the culture who consider themselves avant-garde. When the bourgeoisie react to the provocation, the artist claims that there's no "there" there. After all, sex is natural. There's nothing to get excited about.

And yet, there is something to get excited about and there is a mystery that, however much sex education we unload on our children, cannot—must not—be violated. Human beings seem to have been equipped not only with the sexual urge, but an inability—at least without great struggle—to separate that urge from greater meaning. Indeed, if we judge by the majority of popular songs, finding and achieving a perfect union with one's "soul mate" is the driving goal and purpose of life. In an episode of *The Real World*, the sex-drenched "reality" television show, a young woman agrees with a young man that their relationship will be strictly one of "hooking up"—i.e., sex without attachment. Yet after a couple of hook-ups, the girl is seen crying. Despite her best efforts, her sexual adventure has come with love. In a sad revelation of exactly how far the "pornified" culture has gone in convincing people that sex has nothing to do with the soul, God, or even love, the young woman actually wondered as she wept why she was so upset. The culture of *Playboy*, *Girls Gone Wild*, and Britney Spears had told her that sex was merely recreation. Yet she had formed an attachment. In her soul, she realized that she had given something away. And that something, whether one calls it the heart or the soul, belongs in the realm of the metaphysical. Forty years of pornography and mechanistic sex education have not been able to change that.

Indeed, the "liberated" view of sex that began in the 1950s with *Playboy*—or even as far back as the bohemians of the 1920s—now seems tired, unimaginitive. What has increasingly captured the imagination of young people instead are the traditional views of sex, but given more punch by modern Catholicism. Though we should not ascribe too much real-life influence to a book, *The Theology of the Body* has the potential to free countless young people from the tired—and ironically enslaving— ideas that came with the sexual revolution. It can do so because John Paul II was a thoroughly modern man and probably the most frank of all pontiffs in speaking of human sexuality. In fact, the reality of John Paul II is utterly contrary to his popular image (popular among secular elites, that is) of a repressive prude. This, after all, was the man who, in his 1960 book *Love and Responsibility*, wrote: "[Female frigidity] is usually the result of egoism in the man who, failing to recognize the subjective desires of the woman in intercourse, and the objective laws of the sexual process taking place in her, seeks merely his own satisfaction, sometimes quite brutally."

This was something quite different from the stifling sexual atmosphere of the Catholic Church prior to the 1960s—an atmosphere that has been satirized so relentlessly and for so many decades that it can no longer amuse, but only bore. For decades—or rather centuries—nuns and priests taught ordinary Catholics that the purpose of human sexuality was to bring more souls into the world and thus—hopefully—to heaven. Talk of the process that brought those souls into the world was usually stiff, unimaginative, and pedantic—although not quite as silly as modern liberals claim. It is perhaps fairer to say that for centuries the Catholic Church taught if not falsehoods, then incomplete truths about sex. It was only in the 1920s that certain theologians began to challenge the Church's teachings when they argued that, aside from producing children, the sexual act itself is a totally unique, life altering and sacramental act. Dietrich von Hildebrand insisted in 1968 that the Song of Songs be read not as a metaphor or an analogy of the love of God for the Church, but literally, as an ecstatic love poem and a song of praise for the sexual union between lovers.

It took the Catholic Church until the 1980s to catch up with von Hildebrand. By then, American—and Western—culture had dramatically changed. Many Catholics, having been taught that sex was simply the way to have a lot of children, rebelled against Church teaching. While their use of contraception was an error, their belief that sex in and of itself—and within the bond of marriage—was a wonderful thing was perfectly sound. What was not sound was the sexual propaganda that came out of the media during the sexual revolution of the 1960s as well as the decisions of judges who took over the role of passing the sexual laws of the nation. Americans went from hearing that sex was a word that should not be said aloud to the declaration that sex was not much more complicated or meaningful than exercise. The job of legislating sex went from citizens to judges and, finally, to teachers, journalists, and celebrities.

The great Georgetown University Jesuit James Schall has noted that culture is never neutral. That is to say, certain values will always be encouraged. After the sexual revolution, America did not settle into a neutral position on sex, but rather replaced the old reticence and repression with a new mode of self-expression and a different form of repression—namely, the repression of the enlightened, which taught that curbing the sexual instinct in any way was physically and emotionally unhealthy. While this new ethic considered itself revolutionary, it was—almost—a throwback to the paganism and promiscuity of pre-Christian Rome. Yet there is one essential difference. The theologian Hans Jonas once noted that unlike the "Gnostic man"—the person of the early Christian centuries who disagreed with orthodox Christians that the body was good yet still believed in the soul and a world battling between good and evil—the modern man believes in nothing. Jonas calls this nothingness "an absolute vacuum, the really bottomless pit."

These days it is not enough for conservatives to request that they be left alone. Now there is a desire to convert that is as intense as any sixteenth-century Jesuit missionary's. Dan Savage, a popular syndicated sex columnist, spends an equal amount of time giving advice on various fetishes and condemning conservatives. His columns often combine the red-hot rage of post-1960s liberalism with the cold, impersonal dehumanization and aggressive proselytizing of fascism. In one column he advised a girl who had given up on her chastity pledge. "Take that fucking silver ring thing off your damn finger," he wrote. "You're in college now, cupcake, not high school, and virginity pledges—whether they've been honored or not—will impress precisely none of your new peers." He told the girl to "get a clue," reminding her that "if you're having sex when you're drunk or high, odds are good that you're having sex with other drunk or high people—which means that neither of you consented to the sex, so you raped each other, so you're even."

Contrast it to the words of John Paul II: "The body, in fact, and it alone is capable of making visible what is invisible: the spiritual and divine. It was created to transfer into the visible reality of the world, the mystery hidden since time immemorial in God, and thus to be a sign of it." More than a popular sex columnist, the pontiff of the Roman Catholic Church understands sex—that it is perhaps the most powerful arena of God's action. When that reality is cheapened or destroyed, it causes particular pain in the soul. Furthermore, sex is both a private and public act. No matter what modern liberals say, society has always taken an interest in what we do with our genitals—this has societal as well as metaphysical repercussions. This is the reason for the battle to reclaim sexual virtue. Both souls and civilization are at stake. And the Catholic Church, that old, repressive organization of graying men, offers a way out.

However, it is important that the argument to reclaim what our bodies already know be made with love and reason—and fun. As I was doing research for this work, I was struck with another revelation: The most poetic and powerful expression of the Catholic idea of the nature of love is rock 'n' roll music. I grew up with rock 'n' roll, and as I became a more serious Catholic as I got older I realized that rather than driving me away from Christianity, the music drew me closer. The Beatles and the Rolling Stones (the bands that I grew up with), Coldplay, Van Morrison, Aretha Franklin, and Beyoncé all sing most powerfully about one thing: love. It is the constant, inexhaustible theme of their sounds. If, as the Bible says, God is love, then God must love rock 'n' roll. As I explore in the book, this, of course, does not mean that rock 'n' roll is not rebellious music that challenges social custom. But more often than not, this challenging is a cry for a saner, more just, and moral society, not a more decadent one. Songs by Radiohead, the Rolling Stones, and Bruce Springsteen (and even Mariah Carey) witness to the redemptive power of love and beauty even as they lament the state of the world. They are the opposite of nihilistic.

So while the conservatives are right that Western culture has fallen into a decadence that is often pathological, too many culture warriors are deaf to the musical prayers of the culture and how it relates to God. As rock 'n' roll knows, our defeats may provide important lessons and even a kind of grace. In his book *Jesus of Nazareth*, Pope Benedict XVI wrote the following:

> In order to mature, in order to make real progress on the path leading from a superficial piety into profound oneness with God's will, man needs to be tried. Just as the juice of the grape has to

ferment in order to become a fine wine, so too man needs purifications and transformations. They are dangerous for him, because they present an opportunity to fall. And yet they are indispensable as paths on which he comes to himself and to God.

Or, as the country priest from the novel *The Diary of a Country Priest* by George Bernanos put it: "Blessed is sin if it teaches us shame." It is true that the pornographic liberal culture should be repudiated and exposed as a wellspring of poison and lies that can destroy human souls. But perhaps the most effective way is a gentle revealing of the truth that God has put in every human soul. That is, that sex and love are inseparable, and both constitute perhaps the greatest adventure that mankind has in this world. This simple fact cannot be eradicated by pornographers. They will never be able to destroy what popular songs declare; that is, as one Catholic theologian once put it, in sex, something is given away.

A TREMOR
of BLISS

Chapter One

MY FOOLISH HEART

ON ST. PATRICK'S DAY 2006, THE JAZZ SINGER and former divinity student Kurt Elling preached the theology of the body. The setting was the Strathmore Center, a resplendent $100 million concert hall outside Washington, D.C., and the sermon was in the form of song.

About halfway through the concert, Elling performed the standard "My Foolish Heart." It is a romantic ballad, full of the kind of imagery that goes with love—the nighttime, the moon, the erotic charge of lips. Halfway through the song, the band died down, providing only a slow and steady pulse behind Elling. Then he sang a poem:

One dark night
Fired with love's urgent longings

Clothed in sheer grace
I went out unseen
My house being now all still

On that dark night
Clothed in sheer grace
In darkness and concealed
My house being now all still

On that black night
In secret for no one saw me
With no other light as guide than the one that burned
in my heart
This guided me more surely than the light of noon
To where she waited for me
The one I knew so well
To the place where no one appeared

In the night
In the mystic night

It was a passage from Saint John of the Cross. Elling was commingling the carnal charge of "My Foolish
Heart" with the metaphysical passion of a sixteenth-
century Catholic Spanish mystic. The band was barely
audible, and the space in the concert hall became charged
with a sacramental, erotic energy. After several min-

utes, pianist Laurence Hobgood softly reintroduced the melody to "My Foolish Heart." Elling sang—*"There's a line between love and fascination, it's hard to see on an evening such as this."* The lyrics had returned to the pleasures of kisses and the fire of love, but the distance traveled between Saint John and the Great American Songbook was not far. The band charged back, and the audience of several thousand seemed to both sigh as one and applaud. They—we—had been seduced.

In ten minutes Elling had made the point once made by John Paul II in four years of lectures: To the human person, love recalls the "echo" of our time before the Fall, and as such, our bodily love is an icon of the Trinitarian love of God.

Elling had distilled to its essence *The Theology of the Body.* Based on a series of lectures given between 1979 and 1983 by John Paul II, the book is a theological Mount Everest, considered by most people—including Catholics—too intimidating to approach. Yet at its heart is a fairly simple idea—sex is participation in and a reflection of the love of God; therefore sex, and our bodies themselves, are very good things.

This may seem like an obvious insight—sex has always been associated with the divine. But in the hands of the late pope it reaches remarkable poetic and theological depth. *The Theology of the Body* signaled a sexual revolution in the Catholic Church, one that is now even underway in the larger culture. But it is a revolution that has been more than one hundred years in the making. It is not, obviously, the sexual revolution of the 1960s and perhaps in the larger culture as well, with its shattering "free love" (which, as writer Stephen Catanzarite has pointed out, was neither). Nor is it exactly a conservative counterrevolution. Rather, it is the fulfillment of the thinking of Catholic intellectuals going back to the early twentieth century. These were defenders of sex as something good and holy, freely talking of orgasms and the language of the body at a time when most Catholics were discouraged from even thinking of such things. While their message never trickled down to Catholic schools or stormed the gates of the Vatican, it found powerful expression in the popular culture—particularly in the poetry of rock 'n' roll music. And with John Paul II, it found validation. Now it could be the salvation for Western culture, which has gone sexually insane.

For a time, I was part of that insanity. I was born in 1964 to Irish Catholic parents, and the closest I ever got to a sex talk from my parents was when I was about ten years old. At school I had overheard a teenager call someone a "prick." The next morning, I padded out to the small garden in our backyard where my dad was weeding. "Dad," I asked, "what's a prick?"

For a brief second, he hesitated, his sweaty hands hanging over the tulips. Then he simply started weeding again. It was as though he thought he heard a dog barking in the distance.

I asked again. "What's a prick?"

He weeded.

"Dad," I said again, stepping over the flowerbed so I could not be ignored. "What's a prick?"

He looked at me. Then he gently took me by the shoulders and leaned in close. "It's your penis," he whispered. I felt myself blush. I knew what a penis was. It had to do with sex and we didn't talk about sex. I backed away and retreated into the house while Dad tended to his garden.

Yet my father was the furthest thing from a prude. A journalist and world traveler for *National Geographic*, Dad was brilliant, funny, and passionately loved my mother. The stories he would tell sometimes tended toward the ribald. Once when I pulled a groin muscle playing football, he noticed I was limping around the house. "Were you with a girl last night?" he whispered. I said no, that I had been playing football. "Uh-huh," he said. A devout Catholic, he loved nature and once told my best friend and me that we were being silly when we laughed at two ducks having sex in the backyard. "Hey, it's spring," he said. To Dad, women were magical creatures. He would often become smitten with movie stars and never tired of ballads played by the big bands.

He was, in short, anything but a repressive or hidebound man. Born in 1928, he was of the generation who simply did not talk to their kids about sex—because their parents had not talked to them about sex. We had to find out about sex from other places.

In my case, I learned about love from rock 'n' roll. I still remember the night I fell in love with the Beatles, which was shortly after I had fallen in love with Lisa, the girl next door. It was a hot summer night in 1970, and I was six years old. When I went to bed in our house in Maryland in those days, it was often to the sounds of my oldest brother Joe playing music in his room a few feet down the hall. One night, Joe put on *A Hard Day's Night*, the soundtrack to the great Beatles film.

Many people recall their first experience with the Beatles as cataclysmic, life changing, revolutionary. Like an atomic bomb, the Beatles supposedly destroyed everything that had once stood before, creating the future and a new landscape. Yet on that humid night in 1970, my six-year-old reaction was quite different. I didn't think of war, revolution, my parents, or drugs. I thought of a girl. I thought of Lisa, who lived next door. I was in love with Lisa, and I found that love reflected back to me in the music of *A Hard Day's Night*. In hearing "And I Love Her," "I'm Happy Just to Dance With You," and "If I Fell" from Joe's room, my imagination took off.

The Catholic theologian Fr. Paul M. Quay would later describe the sexual act as a woman opening herself up to a man, her giving of herself, and the man penetrating her with his very essence—put simply, their mutual self-giving—an expression of the love of God. Though I wasn't remotely conscious of it at the time, John, Paul, George, and Ringo offered the same message. Like intense and very effective prayer, you could feel God in their sound—the happy bounce of "I Should Have Known Better"; the mystical, hopeful solemnity of "Things We Said Today"; the orgasmic cries of "When I Get Home." In those brilliant notes, I saw Lisa and me dancing, laughing, kissing, being husband and wife. If this was revolutionary music, it was preaching a very old lesson: the power of love.

I soon realized that love—and its loss—is the great theme of popular music, from Louis Armstrong right down to Justin Timberlake. Popular music was exploring the initial ecstasy Adam felt when he first saw "flesh of my flesh and bone of my bone." Whether it was the Supremes declaring there ain't no mountain high enough, the Beatles heralding the good news that she loves you, or Van Morrison whispering about a marvelous night for a moondance, this great desire to return to our original union with God—including the conjugal union between Adam and Eve that preceded the Fall—is the urge that launched a thousand hits.

Indeed, it is such a ubiquitous theme that it's impossible to run through my favorite bands without coming face-to-face with it. The punk group the Replacements, my favorite band when I was in my twenties, have a song called "I Will Dare," about working up the courage to meet a girl. The Allman Brothers sing of "Sweet Melissa." The entire Motown canon, from Marvin Gaye to Stevie Wonder, is a joyful soundtrack of the quest for love—more specifically, the quest for the love of that one person you were meant to be with, the one who is the answer to a prayer, who can make time stop.

In his encyclical *Deus Caritas Est* ("God Is Love"), Pope Benedict XVI refers to the love between a man and a woman as "that love which is neither planned nor willed, but somehow imposes itself upon human beings." In the U2 song "Original of the Species," singer Bono says that love "steals right under my door," neither planned nor willed. Bono can only cry for more, delirious with the fecundity and gratuitous grace of God. It's probably no mistake, given his acknowledged Catholic spirituality, that he cries "I want you some more" three times, perhaps reflecting the Trinity.

Of course, the Beatles could not teach me the basics of reproductive biology. I also wasn't going to get that in Catholic parochial school. In the 1970s my grade school, Our Lady of Mercy in Maryland, was not ready for the sexual revolution. The school was run by two women—Sister Mary, the principal, and Miss Donahue (not their real names), a teacher who would eventually become principal. Both women were tough yet fair; both were feared and respected by the students. Unlike my father, they could not joke about sex. Like any boy with a crush, I found myself obsessing about Lisa during class. Sister Mary or Miss Donahue would be dilating about the nature of angels or conjugating verbs, and I would stare out the window, fantasizing about kissing Lisa.

Finally, one afternoon I was on the street playing wiffle ball when Lisa came walking by on her way home from school. Inspired by "I Wanna Hold Your Hand," I asked her if I could kiss her.

She said yes.

I stood there. We watched each other for a few seconds. Then she turned and walked home. I had lost my nerve.

For the rest of the summer I was slowly tortured by my inaction—but I was also inspired. Lisa had said I could kiss her. All I had to do was do it.

The moment came when school began a few weeks later. I was playing catch with a friend when she came by on her way home from school. She was about to pass by when I spoke up: "Um . . . Lisa? Can I kiss you now?"

"OK."

I moved in. At the last second she turned, making sure I hit her on the cheek and not the mouth.

For the next several days, I was in a dream world. Sister Mary and Miss Donahue talked multiplication tables and transubstantiation, but only my physical body was in class. I was already married to Lisa, or reliving the kiss over and over again. There was simply nobody in school or at home who could explain to me why I felt the way I did. When I mentioned Lisa, my dad just smiled. I graduated from Our Lady of Mercy in the spring of 1979 having kissed a girl, but still not knowing much about what the rock musician Elvis Costello, who had just hit the charts with his first album, called the "Mystery Dance."

Things would be explained to me, graphically, when I got to high school. I went to Georgetown Prep, the little brother school to Georgetown University. Apparently by this time the Catholic Church had gotten over its reticence about sex. Our sex-ed teacher at Prep was a man named Bernie Ward, who would later become a well-known left-wing talk show host in San Francisco. Ward would also be arrested and convicted for sending pornographic images of children over the Internet.

On the first day of sex-ed class, Ward, an average-sized man with a bad complexion, handed out the day's reading—a tract about feminism and sex by Betty Friedan. He then went to the front of the classroom and made an announcement: There was nothing wrong with masturbation. It was healthy. It was normal. It would make you happy. In fact, masturbating, even if you were married, would only help the relationship. For the next six months, the female body became a sort of flesh-and-bone vending machine, something that would respond and deliver if you knew where to insert the quarter and pushed the right button.

Mr. Ward's exegesis on sex did not do me much

good when I lost my virginity the summer after I took his class. I met Donna when I had a party when I was seventeen and my parents were out of town. The kids left the house a mess, and Donna and a friend had stayed behind to help me clean up. It was about two a.m. when we were finishing, and as Donna was vacuuming up beer I pulled her toward me and kissed her. Mr. Ward had filled my vocabulary with words like clitoris, orgasm, and ejaculation. What he hadn't prepared me for was falling in love with a real person. To be sure, hormones were driving me to have sex with Donna. But it was also something more transcendent. As Saint Ambrose once put it, lovers embracing seem to be attempting to breathe their souls into each other.

Again, rock 'n' roll seemed to describe the powerful parallel world I was entering. Where my parents and their generation considered lovemaking a wonderful taboo not to be spoken of in detail, and Mr. Ward reduced it to Marxism and moving parts, the songs I loved told me that it could be both—the swiveling hips of Elvis and the tender ballads of the Fab Four; the erotic dynamism of Little Richard and the moonlit romance of Van Morrison. To put it in theological terms, the music made the connection between agape, the love of God, and eros, physical desire. At night, from Joe's room, Jimi Hendrix, the Rolling Stones, the Allman Brothers, and the blues musicians he loved would serenade me with the wonder of love.

Yet the Church was catching up with the Top 40. In September 1979—my first week at Georgetown Prep—Pope John Paul II began a series of lectures that would be published as *The Theology of the Body*. John Paul II went back to Genesis to reveal the true meaning of love and the human body. The pope emphasized that man—meaning all human persons—was made in the image of God. Thus, when we are seeing another person, we are seeing the image of God. We become even more like God through the act of loving that person as an image of God, not as an object of lust. And we can only achieve mastery of ourselves and our sexuality by realizing that we ourselves are also created in the image of God. When we know this fully, we can come to realize genuine freedom.

The Theology of the Body had its origin in early 1940, when a nineteen-year-old Polish seminarian named Karol Wojtyla met Jan Tyranowski, a thirty-nine-year-old tailor living in Krakow, which had been taken over by the Nazis. The Germans had stripped Poland of much of its Catholic clergy, and as a result many Catholics were forced underground, where they sought instruction and inspiration from laymen. One of the most charismatic of these was Tyranowski.

As a teenager, Tyranowski had heard a sermon in which the priest declared, "It's not difficult to be a saint." Smitten by the phrase, Tyranowski took a vow of celibacy and organized his life around religious practice and reading. He was soon a genuine Catholic mystic. In the words of theologian George Weigel, for Tyranowski, "the goal of contemplative prayer was a release from thoughts and images, a freedom to simply be in God's presence."

After the Gestapo sent Polish priests to concentration camps, Tyranowski formed an underground Catholic group called the Living Rosary, made up of groups of young men who devoted themselves to spiritual development and mutual support. Wojtyla soon became a leader of this group. Tyranowski's example, he later recalled, "proved that one could not only inquire about God but that one could live with God." It was Tyranowski who introduced Wojtyla to Saint John of the Cross, the sixteenth-century Catholic mystic. Wojtyla, an athlete as well as a scholar who had seen several friends fall in love, was struck by the love poetry of Saint John, who drew a direct correlation between physical experience and the love of God. In works like "The Ascent of Mount Carmel" and "The Dark Night of the Soul," Saint John combines poetry and prose in an ecstatic ode to union with the Lord:

O lamps of fire!
in whose splendors
the deep caverns of feeling

once obscure and blind,
now give forth, so rarely, so exquisitely,
both warmth and light to their Beloved.

In his commentary on the last two lines, Saint John writes that "since God gives himself with a free and gracious will, so too the soul (possessing a will more generous and free the more it is united with God) gives to God, God himself in God; and this is a true and complete gift of the soul to God."

A reciprocal love is thus actually formed between God and the soul, like the marriage union and surrender, in which the goods of both (the divine essence that each possesses freely by reason of the voluntary surrender between them) are possessed by both together. They say to each other what the Son of God spoke to the Father through John: All that is mine is yours and yours is mine, and I am glorified in them [Jn. 17:10].

The young Wojtyla became so smitten with John of the Cross that he wrote his dissertation on the Spanish mystic. The future pope would emphasize the Trinitarian aspect of the union between the soul and God—that is to say, the love of God was mirrored in human love, especially human sexual love. Wojtyla: "This concept of the relationship between God and the soul, at once filial and conjugal, is based on two constant elements: [1] the adoptive communication of grace and [2] the power of love." The soul, Wojtyla wrote, becomes "God by participation" and therefore by participation it possesses divinity itself.

The theologian Michael Waldstein has noted three "points of contact" between John of the Cross and John Paul II. They are "(1) Love implies a cycle of mutual giving, supremely the gift of self. (2) The paradigmatic instance of such self-gift in human experience is the spousal relation between man and woman. (3) The Trinity is the archetype of such love and gift from which the love between God and human persons as well as love between human beings derives as an imitation and participation." Saint John, Waldstein writes, "describes the soul's relation to God as a cycle of mutual giving. The deep satisfaction and happiness of love is found in this cycle as a cycle of giving, not only of receiving (see TOB 68:2–3)." Saint John speaks of man and woman in union, and of the bride as giving herself:

There he gave me his breast;
there he taught me a sweet and living knowledge;
and I gave myself to him,
keeping nothing back;
there I promised to be his bride.

The characteristic feature of the spousal love between human beings and God is the totality of the gift of self, which is reflected in the totality of the orientation of affections toward the spouse. "I gave myself to him, keeping nothing back; there I promised to be his bride." "Spiritual marriage," Waldstein observes, "is the total surrendering of the self-possession of each to the other, analogous to the consummation of love by sexual union in marriage." As Wojtyla wrote:

> Betrothed [spousal] love differs from all the aspects or forms of love analyzed hitherto. Its decisive character is the giving of one's own person (to another). This is something different from and more than attraction, desire, or even good will. These are all ways by which one person goes out toward another, but none of them can take him as far. . . . The fullest, the most uncompromising form of love consists precisely in self-giving, in making one's inalienable and non-transferable "I" someone else's property.

It's hardly surprising that on his deathbed, John of the Cross wanted to hear not prayers for those about to die, but the Song of Songs.

For much of the Church's history, theologians were unsure how to interpret the Song of Songs, a book that can only be described as sexy. It is also the book that has generated more commentaries than any other in the history of the Church. The Song of Songs is a poem spilling over with the joy of physical love. It is fulsome with metaphor.

From the Bride:

My beloved is mine and I am his.
He pastures his flock among the lilies.
Before the dawn wind raises,
Before the shadows flee,
Return! Be, my beloved,
Like a gazelle,
A young stag,
On the mountains of the covenant.
On my bed, at night, I sought him whom my heart
*   loves.*
I sought him but did not find him.
So I will rise and go through the city;
In the streets and the squares
I will seek him whom my heart loves
. . . I sought but did not find him.

The Bridegroom replies:

How beautiful you are, my love,
How beautiful you are!
Your eyes behind your veil,
Are doves;
Your hair is like a flock of goats

Frisking down the slopes of Gilead.
Your teeth are like a flock of shorn ewes
As they come up from the washing.
Each one has its twin,
Not one unpaired with another.
Her lips are a scarlet thread
And your words enchanting.
Your cheeks, behind your veil,
Are halves of pomegranate.
Your neck is the tower of David
Built as a fortress,
Hung around with a thousand bucklers,
And each the shield of a hero.
Your two breasts are two fawns,
Twins of a gazelle,
That feed among the lilies.

For virtually all of Church history, the Song of Songs was considered an allegory of the love of God for His people. Origen, Saint Basil, and Saint Gregory of Nyssa in the third century; Ambrose in the fourth century; and Saint Augustine and Saint Gregory the Great in the seventh century all interpreted the song in the same way. At the Fifth Council of Constantinople in 533, they condemned the proposition, held by Theodore of Mopsuestia and not many others, that the song was a purely secular poem. As one scholar put it, "The free love of Song celebrates only one thing: The splendid, radiant, and terrifying glory of eros between man and woman. Eros itself vibrates without any other purpose than natural love. . . . Eros is sufficient unto itself. The eros of the Song is not the agape of God."

In 1983 the Jesuit Blaise Arminjon, in his book *The Cantata of Love*, examined the Song of Songs from all the different angles. He concludes that the Song is holy not despite being erotic, even carnal, but because it is those things. "There is apparently no concern for theology, apologetics, teaching or morality," Arminjon wrote. "Contrary to all the other books in the Bible . . . the tone of the Song is so passionate, even so daring here and there, and it makes such an appeal to the senses (to all the senses), that it is difficult to see how it could be suitable to the expression of God's love. The love of the bridegroom and his bride is that of beings made of flesh and blood."

Mystics throughout Church history have particularly embraced the Song. When he was seventeen in 1584, Saint Francis de Sales took a course in Paris on the Song, and it became his favorite book. Saint Catherine of Siena and Saint Teresa of Avila both adored the Song of Songs. And yet, throughout Church history, there was also suspicion of the Song. Saint Gregory the Great made this assessment: "In order to inflame our hearts to His sacred love, (God) goes as far as using the language of our crude love and, stooping thus in his words, he raises up our understanding. Indeed, it is through the language of this love that we learn how strongly we must burn with divine love."

Saint Gregory of Nyssa actually advised that "when we want to devote ourselves to contemplation [of the Song], forget thoughts related to marriage . . . so that, having extinguished all carnal appetites, it will be only through the Spirit that our intelligence will simmer lovingly, warmed by the fire that the Lord has come to bring on earth." Saint Bernard of Clairvaux preached, "One cannot start reading this book unless he has reached a certain degree of purity. Any other reading would be unworthy if the flesh had not been tamed, if it had not yet been submitted to the Spirit by exacting discipline." When he describes this sermon, Blaise Arminjon imagines in the audience "a small Cistercian novice, still callous and poorly initiated in the Word of Wisdom, quite new to the science of love." Despite that, he is "listening to the words of the Abbot with delight. He does not bother to ask himself whether he has reached the necessary degree of purity and maturity. Quite simply: He is happy."

Here is real insight into the Song of Songs and its power. Instinctively, in our conscience and beneath official dogma and theology, we know that there is something holy in our bodies and their sexual expression—that in casting our eyes on the wonderful features of the beloved, we are casting our eyes toward heaven—or, as John Paul II would have it in *The Theology of the Body*, casting our eyes back to the very beginning, when Adam and Eve lived untainted by sin. I had felt it when I kissed Lisa for the first time. I felt it when I touched Donna.

In his biography of Saint John of the Cross, Crisógono De Jesús tells of the great mystic on his deathbed. "Tell me about the Song of Songs," Saint John told the Carmelites who had started to read the prayers for the recommendation of the soul. "This other thing is of no use to me."

Kurt Elling and the Fab Four might have said the same thing. And Lisa and Donna.

Chapter Two

YEAR ZERO

ONE NIGHT IN THE SUMMER OF 2007, I MADE a pass at a woman I met out dancing. The woman was from India, growing up in Ahmedabad in the western part of the country before coming to the United States in 2003. We danced together and started talking. She was funny, smart, and beautiful.

At the end of the night, I walked her to her car. When I tried to kiss her good night, she turned away. I apologized, saying I had maybe gotten wrong signals, and started to turn to go home. "Wait," she said. Then she took my head in her hands and kissed me three times—once on each cheek and then on the forehead. Then she said I could call her.

There is a moment in Jack London's book *John Barleycorn* when he describes getting drunk for the first time. London was just a child. His father was working in the fields and asked for a pail of beer. Jack's mother filled it and sent her son out to make the short trip. On the way, young London stopped to take a few drinks. Soon he felt a warmth creep over his body. He felt giddy, "like a guitar string that had been plucked." When I was kissed on my forehead and cheeks, I also felt like a plucked guitar string. Or, to use another literary example, I felt like protagonist Jamie at the end of Jay McInerney's book *Bright Lights, Big City.* Having nearly destroyed himself with drugs, sex, and drink, Jamie exchanges his expensive sunglasses for a piece of bread. "You must learn to do everything all over again," he tells himself.

Sexually, America needs to learn to do everything all over again. The American obsession with sex has made us less sexual. The incessant sexual themes and jokes on our sitcoms, the emphasis on condoms and human plumbing in the schools, the magazines that are always promising better, more explosive sex, the tape loop of erectile dysfunction ads on television—the overall effect is one that deadens the senses rather than enriches them. Studies have shown that excessive viewing of pornography initiates a need for ever-higher escalation of graphic images, eventually making it impossible for a person to achieve sexual arousal. It's like pitching in major league baseball games four days in a row. Eventually the body, and the soul, just crashes.

There is a tradition going back at least to Saint

Augustine of sexual sinners repenting and becoming self-righteous exemplars of purity. The world does not need another one of those accounts in detail, which is why, in this work, I only touch on my own experience tangentially. It's probably enough to say that I slept around when I was younger. I was no different from many Americans.

However, there is a moment I still think of. In the 1980s I became a journalist like my father, and I spent most of my time working on articles and books. When I wasn't working, I was partying, going to concerts and trips to the beach, and looking to hook up with women. At one point I had a fling with a woman, Ellen, who worked in a bar in Georgetown, the adult playground in Washington, D.C. I would meet her in the late hours at the end of her shift and we would talk and laugh and drink beer, then go back to her apartment or mine and make love. Once when I came to see her, she was the only one left in the bar. The place had once been a house and it was large, with two floors and a back terrace that was enclosed in glass and offered a view of Georgetown's streets. Ellen locked the front door and took me by the hand to the back terrace. We made love on the floor, but also—I think because during our passion I had backed against a door—set off a silent alarm that rang at the police station. The police soon arrived, followed by the owner. Ellen mumbled something about an accident, and we escaped.

About a month later, we stayed up all night drinking in the bar. Standing on M Street, the main strip in Georgetown, and watching the early morning light color the red brick row houses and bars and shops, she said she had something to tell me. She had gotten pregnant and had had an abortion.

I offered her my sympathy and support. I told her that I wished she had told me earlier, so I could have offered her some consolation.

We parted, and never slept together again.

At the time, and for years afterwards, I told myself that Ellen's abortion was no big deal. I was a disciple in the Church of Mr. Ward and condom-loving modern America. Only fascists were pro-life. And only prudes wanted to control sex.

Yet in a small corner of my heart, I wept. I knew that something catastrophic had happened with Ellen. It was the disastrous result of my promiscuity, the deadly end point of a narcissism that puts the sexual self and its satisfaction at the top of a hierarchy of values: sex, self-expression, freedom to do whatever one wants no matter what the consequences. And deep hatred for purity.

After all, I was born in 1964 and had grown up in the era of "Punitive Liberalism." That phrase comes from James Piereson and his remarkable book *Camelot and the Cultural Revolution: How the Assassination of John F. Kennedy Shattered American Liberalism*. Piereson's thesis is that the liberal establishment dealt with the assassination of President Kennedy in 1963 by, first, blaming it on the wrong people, and second, becoming paranoid, punitive, conspiratorial, and anti-American. Lee Harvey Oswald was a Castro-sympathizing communist who murdered Kennedy, an atrocity that exploded liberal arguments that had downplayed the threat of communism. Instead of facing this, liberals pivoted, shifting the blame for Kennedy's death onto racist rednecks in Texas and the "larger climate of hate" that had become part of America. "I want them to see what they have done," Jackie Kennedy said, refusing in the immediate aftermath of the assassination to change her bloody clothes.

As Piereson writes, the "they" she—and the media—referred to were the violent, reactionary, racists of the United States. The day after the assassination, James Reston wrote this in the *New York Times*: "America weeps tonight, not alone for its dead young president, but for itself. The grief was general, for somehow the worst in the nation had prevailed over the best. The indictment extended beyond the assassin, for something in the nation itself, some strain of madness and violence, had destroyed the highest symbol of law and order." Piereson observes that Reston "seems to have reached an instinctive conclusion about the cause of the event without any reference to the actual identity of the assassin." Before Kennedy's murder, liberalism had been the dominant political ideology in America. But unlike the "progressive" far left, which criticized Kennedy and other practical liberals for lacking boldness and imagination, American liberalism before Kennedy's death was optimistic, anti-communist, sexually modest (at least in public), and patriotic. It was programmatic. It believed in progress, but progress that did not cause too much upheaval and was achieved in order to make America better and stronger. It wanted to extend the New Deal but not go nuts about it. Kennedy was slow in getting involved with the Civil Rights Movement while at the same time cutting taxes and confronting the Russians in Cuba. Kennedy referred to himself as "a liberal without illusions."

He was also a bulwark against the passions of the progressive left as well as the lunatic far right. In the 1950s and early 1960s, a group of what Christopher Lasch called "the new radicals" had emerged. Their goal was no longer, as it had been with the old progressives, to fight capitalism in the name of populism and democracy, but to attack cultural foundations: the family, education, sex ("especially sex," Lasch noted). On the other side, the far right was infected with paranoia, resentment, and anti-Americanism. Birchers warned of fluoridation in the water and condemned America for being communist. Liberal historians such as Richard Hofstadter and Arthur Schlesinger used the far right to indict all of conservatism—although, as P³ Piereson notes, the "vital center" of liberalism distrusted passionate ideology of both the far left and far right. "If the Progressive historians had viewed American history as a continuing battle between capitalism and democracy," Pierson notes, "Hofstadter and his liberal colleagues portrayed a different kind of conflict, one in which the national psyche was divided between a commitment to liberal rationality on the one side and the temptation to engage in emotional and counterproductive tantrums on the other."

When Kennedy died, liberals performed a reconstruction that discarded the real JFK. Kennedy's timidity on civil rights was forgotten, as was his dislike of the far left. No one talked about his support of Joseph McCarthy or his criticism of Harry Truman for not being enough of an anti-communist. No one mentioned his huge tax cuts. Pierson: "Kennedy, through his life and death, had somehow managed to change the terms of American liberalism from a doctrine of programmatic reform with an emphasis on economic security and national defense to one of cultural change and criticism with an emphasis on liberation and the reform of traditional morals and ways of living."

The New Left arrived, and with it what Pierson brilliantly calls the era of "Punitive Liberalism." Punitive liberalism was different from programmatic liberalism, which Kennedy exemplified. Punitive liberalism was angry at the United States and sought to punish her. The rednecks in Texas had killed Kennedy, so they should be written out of politics. Profits were wrong, and Christians were illiterate and uptight. If one person was suffering, it was a crisis that reflected badly on us and needed to be addressed right now. Marriage was a patriarchal trap. America was not a flawed but essentially good country; it was a malevolent colossus that needed to be brought down. Looking to the future with hope was replaced by the idea that a golden age, Camelot, was lost, and there was no going back. Punitive liberalism was more interested in assigning blame for our racist, greedy, homophobic country than creating any actual programs that might work. Punitive liberalism became what the far right of the previous era had been: paranoid, frustrated, given to hysterical rhetoric, fearful of the future, and anti-American. Punitive liberalism wasn't utopian; it was—is—narcissistic and punishing.

This is why the modern sexual "liberators" are not content to preach their wordview—they must vanquish the bourgeois enemy. A few blocks from where John Kennedy had lived in Washington, D.C., when he was a senator is Georgetown University, a putatively Catholic university and the big brother to Georgetown Prep, my alma mater. In February 2010—indeed, during Lent—the university held "Sex Positive Week." It was a meeting of students and speakers promoting S&M, homosexuality, anal sex, and a general openness about all things sexual. Speakers included an anal sex expert and there was a talk about various sex toys. In Red Square, an open space in the center of campus, one student loudly delivered a monologue about the clitoris to students passing by. It is noteworthy that this student did not feel it was enough to have premarital sex, or gay sex, or sadomasochistic sex, in private. It was not enough to advocate acceptance of these things among similar aficionados. No, it was necessary to change those around her. She had to literally scream in their faces. This was quintessential punitive liberalism.

Sadly, it has been going on at Georgetown for years. In 2005, one would have found numerous copies of *Current*, a glossy magazine distributed to colleges and universities around the country. It is, as the title blurb says, "for college students, by college students." Call it a farm system for the mainstream media. The above-the-title headline on that fall's cover: SPECIAL GUIDE TO A PIMPED-OUT ROOM. The article offered instructions on how to decorate your dorm room to make a street-walker proud. Another article, "Sexpionage," encouraged women to, well, act like prostitutes. "Raised on HBO softcore porn and Janet Jackson music videos, the modern woman has appropriated the proverbial pants in the mating ritual." It is time, author Anna Ritner proclaims, "to wage a subversive war on courtship." Leaf past *Current*'s obligatory genuflecting to "diversity"—a forum by college newspaper editors on whether their campuses are "multi-culti" enough—and there's a piece on contraception. Author Victoria Bosch—a Georgetown student—describes a friend who was thrilled when "her long-time lust object asked her out." Despite Georgetown being surrounded by drugstores, the girl couldn't get contraception: "As a student at a conservative school affiliated with a mainstream religion, she would not have been able to procure emergency contraception from the student health center. Too scared to go to Planned Parenthood, she had asked me to pick up the prescription." In case you're not getting it, the next paragraph leaves no doubt: "My friend's religious college did not keep her from gettin' down. It did, however, make her situation more dangerous." Is it possible that such thinking promotes risky behavior? Not according to Jack Trussell at Princeton University. He cites six studies to Bosch. No need to find a dissenting voice.

A few pages later one finds a full spread titled "Here Come the Brides," about gay marriage. Carolina Oster and Sylvia Glassco at Yale "met in marching band and fostered a relationship." At the Harvard-Yale game, even alumni sent congratulations—"It seemed like no one could get enough of the young couple." Of course, simply recounting these facts is good journalism, so I knew there had to be more—the indispensable shot at conservatives: "Even critics of same-sex marriage can't help contracting the couple's contagious enthusiasm."

According to Glassco, "A good friend of ours who is very conservative said to me, 'Sylvia, I'm opposed to gay marriage, you know that. But I want good people to be married.'"

One may observe that Chrissy A. Balz, a student at Georgetown and the writer of "Here Come the Brides," did not do her job by failing to interview those who were not charmed by Oster and Glassco, or that Victoria Bosch fumbled her contraception piece by not noting any dissenters from the *Playboy* culture (*Playboy* has a half-page ad in *Current*), or that promoting a pimped-out room in a magazine distributed on a Catholic university campus is in poor taste. But *Current* is published by *Newsweek*. It's a warm-up for big-time journalism. It is crucial that these kids learn to ignore sources they disagree with.

Of course, in the end it's all dreadfully dull, lacking the snap and crackle of those poor repressed students, with their manners and morals and faith, in pre-1960s America. G. K. Chesterton once remarked that it's easy for a dead fish to go with the current, but it takes something alive to go against it. Reading *Current* is like watching dead fish float by. The social critic Ross Douthat once observed that liberals like to assume that almost everything prior to the 1960s in America was a dark age. The sexual left likes to play to the media and satisfy their egos by creating a sense that they are keepers of the enlightenment and all things good—by "setting a year zero somewhere around 1970 and casting everything that's happened since as a battle between progress and atavism, reason and fundamentalism, the enlightenment and the medieval dark." Such a battle is indeed taking place, and the forces of atavism are the neo-Gnostics of modern culture. Strange as it may seem, magazines like *Current, Cosmopolitan, Playboy, Redbook,* and *Elle,* which are always promising to reveal "the secret" to better orgasms, fantastic sex in bed, or the ten ways to drive your mate wild, would not have been out of place at the beginnings of Christianity. Such magazines reflect the Gnosticism of the early Church. Gnosticism was a heretical movement of early Christianity—although some scholars hold that it existed even before the birth of Christ—which held that matter was evil, including human sexuality. Gnostics believed that the divine was attainable through a "saving knowledge" that others did not have. Because the Gnostics were dualists, believing that matter—including the human body—is evil, they argued that sex should take place only among the unenlightened, that its goal should be strictly for pleasure, and that contraception should be used.

While the Church fathers disputed the Gnostics—Saint Irenaeus wrote that Gnostics who found fault with marriage were "implicitly finding fault with Him who made human beings male and female so that they could reproduce"—they sometimes seemed as negative about sex as the Gnostics themselves. In the second century Saint Justin Martyr wrote, "We Christians either marry with but one thought, to beget children, or, if we refuse to marry, we are completely continent." Saint Clement of Alexandria and Athenagoras of Athens both opined that the purpose of marriage is children. Church fathers Saint Gregory of Nyssa, Saint John Chrysostom, Saint Theodoret, and Saint John Damascene actually believed that sexual desire was a result of the Fall. They held that God originally had a plan for people to have children without having sex, but knowing that the fall from paradise would occur, had also given Adam and Eve genitals.

The early Christians may have had difficulty finding a place in their cosmology for sexual desire because, while they were resisting the Gnostics on one side, on the other was Greco-Roman paganism, which they regarded as irredeemably licentious and corrupt—awash in disregard for life, as well as prostitution, divorce, infanticide, and contraception. In rebuffing the Gnostics, early Christians did not want to be seen as embracing the pagans. Out of this crucible came Saint Augustine, the fifth-century saint whose writings about sex would be profoundly influential in the Church. Augustine had conflicting and even contradictory views about sex, and was not nearly the prude that some have made him out to be. Indeed, many of his views on sex are grounded in natural law and scripture and are still upheld by the Church. Augustine felt that original sin caused humans to lose their reason to pursue short-term desires. Yet the grace of Christ enables a restoration—we can fulfill our desires as long as we do so in a way that is ordered toward God, the ultimate good. Augustine argued that sex provided three goods: children, fidelity, and indissoluble unity. Children were new souls who had been called to a life for God. However, "Intercourse for the purpose of satisfying concupiscence, provided it is with a spouse, is but venial fault because of fidelity. Adultery or fornication, however, is a mortal sin." In other words, marriage promoted fidelity and thus the avoidance of fornication and adultery; but simply having sex to quell lust without any other good in mind is a venial sin. What Augustine misses, as theologians Ronald Lawler, Joseph Boyle, and William May note in their book *Catholic Sexual Ethics*, is that a couple may choose to have sex not to alleviate lust, but to show fidelity. "Augustine does not explicitly entertain the possibility that both spouses might choose marital relations as a way of showing their fidelity, their love." The third good of marriage was the bond of indissoluble unity between husband and wife. The sacrament of marriage had been instituted by Christ himself, and those who partook in it received gifts of grace. Marriage is touched by and a reflection of the bond between Christ and His Church.

Augustine's philosophy was the rule of the Church

for centuries, until it was developed further by medieval theologians such as Saint Thomas Aquinas and Saint Bonaventure in the thirteenth century. Aquinas held that sex for the sake of fidelity is good. Aquinas, who wrote so compellingly about pleasure and the role of the senses in feeling the presence of God, agreed with Aristotle that pleasure is part of the perfection of the human being—although Aquinas never denied that lust for pleasure was sinful. The point was to treat sex and its pleasures as a sacrament and a way to express faithfulness, friendship, and love.

Aquinas faced resurgent neo-Gnostic movements of the High Middle Ages, metaphysical religious movements like Catharism, Bogomilism, and Albigensianism. Arising in the twelfth century, the Cathars, who called themselves "The Pure," rejected procreation. As one clergyman noted, "They say it is as great a crime to enter into one's wife as into one's mother or daughter." According to one witness, the Cathars called sex "the forbidden fruit." Nonetheless, they did not oppose the wedding ceremony. One clergyman wrote to Pope Lucius II in 1145 that the Cathars "fictitiously communicate in our sacraments to veil their wickedness."

For the next seven centuries, the Catholic Church's teachings about sex did not change. Indeed, they were hardly even challenged. Marriage was considered a good; adultery, fornication, homosexuality, masturbation, and bestiality gravely sinful. This began to change in the twentieth century. Most people date the start of the sexual revolution to the 1960s, but it really began much earlier, in the 1920s, which is why *Time* magazine referred to the new libertinism as "the second sexual revolution." Following World War I, a new breed of young bohemians, or "bright young things," had challenged the straightlaced Victorian morality of their parents.

In the October 30, 1926, edition of the Jesuit magazine *America*, Fr. Raymond J. Gray, S.J., wrote about "the younger set"—and he was not optimistic. "Judges, social workers, and teachers have in despair appealed to parents to exercise a more severe watch over their children," Gray wrote. "Especially do they insist on the absolute necessity of teaching the young habits of self-restraint, of respect for maturity, and of a proper evaluation of those moral and religious motives without which self-conquest is nearly impossible." The young were interested in parties, movies, spending money—and sex. In this they were encouraged by the elites of their time. What is remarkable is how some of these names are still venerated by liberals, despite the absurdity—and even brutality—of some of their ideas.

Margaret Sanger is revered by modern feminists as the founder of Planned Parenthood. In her article entitled "The Woman Rebel," Sanger expressed her creed this way: "A woman's duty: To look the whole world in the face with a go-to-hell look in the eyes, to have an ideal, to speak and act in defiance of convention."

This means advocating "free love" and contraception. Free love was the original hook-up ethos. It called for sex without emotional commitment. Sanger's push for contraception was based on the new theology of eugenics, which held that it was necessary for certain races to make sure other "inferior" races did not breed too much. Sanger, a thoroughly enlightened progressive, wanted to create "a race of thoroughbreds" by eliminating "the dead weight of human waste." More important, perhaps, Sanger was one of the first people to claim that Christian virtues, or even the attempt to achieve them, actually had the opposite effect: "Out of the unchallenged policies of continence, abstinence, chastity, and purity, we have reaped the harvests of prostitution, venereal scourges, and innumerable other evils."

Sanger then announced the mantra that would become the slogan of liberal sex educators for the next hundred years and counting. "The great central problem, and one which must be taken first is the abolition of the shame and fear of sex." Anticipating such modern liberationists as Eve Ensler and Larry Flynt, Sanger saw sex as the key to human liberation. "Through sex, mankind may attain the great spiritual illumination which will transform the world, which will light up the only path to an earthly paradise. So must we necessarily and inevitably conceive of sex expression."

With missionary zeal, Sanger and Planned Parenthood soon set out to change the Comstock laws that outlawed the sale and use of contraceptives. These repressive laws were the handiwork of Anthony Comstock, a prominent anti-smut crusader who lived from 1844 to 1915. Probably the truest thing ever said about Comstock came from the pen of H. L. Mencken, who noted upon his death, "He did more than any man to ruin Puritanism in the United States." Like the liberal sex educators and free-love gurus who conquered America in the 1960s, Comstock was a tyrant who lacked common sense. The son of a wealthy New England farmer, he had fought for the Union side in the Civil War. Scandalized by the language and behavior of some of his fellow soldiers, he tried to organize a temperance society and called for prayer meetings.

Comstock moved to New York in 1871. At the time the city was lively with prostitution, gambling, and pornography. In 1872 Comstock formed the New York Society for the Suppression of Vice. In its first year 194,000 pictures, 60,300 "rubber articles," and sixty-seven tons of books were destroyed. But this was not enough to stop the burgeoning flood of pornography. In 1873 he cleverly attacked the problem through the passage of a federal law against using the mail for the sale of such explicit materials. The law read, in part, that "every filthy book, pamphlet, picture, letter, writing, print, or other publication of an indecent character, and every article or thing designated, adapted, or intended for preventing conception or procuring abortion, for any indecent or immoral use . . . is hereby declared to be non-mailable matter." Fines could be levied up to five thousand dollars or five years in prison. After the law's passage, Comstock became special agent to the Office of the Postmaster General. He was a dictator of the postal service with the power to inspect any piece of mail he wanted and to arrest, without warrant, anyone who sent something through the mail of which he disapproved. He openly bragged that he had caused several people to commit suicide. The socialist playwright George Bernard Shaw created the phrase "Comstockery" to refer to all such attempts at puritanical repression.

Sanger and Planned Parenthood adopted a two-pronged approach to getting their views on sex accepted by a conservative Christian America. The first was an attack on the Comstock laws through the courts, medical organizations, and social workers. In 1936, Sanger arranged for a package of contraceptives to be sent through the mail to Dr. Hannah Stone, a physician in a Planned Parenthood clinic. When she accepted the package, she was charged with violating the Comstock law. The case went to trial and after an initial conviction, Dr. Stone won on appeal, the three-judge federal court ruling that the law should not apply to "the importation, sale, or carriage of things which might be employed by conscientious and competent physicians for the purpose of saving life or promoting the well-being of their patients."

It was the first step in what would be the slow and steady encroachment of birth control into the country by working around legislatures. (The Comstock laws themselves would be overturned in 1973.) In March 1934, a Senate subcommittee held a hearing on S. 1842, another of Sanger's proposals for medical birth control. Sanger cited the experience of Weld County, Colorado, in using birth control to reduce welfare costs, alleging that for $300 spent on birth control for two hundred women, some $10,000 in public expenditures were saved. A Catholic priest, Fr. John Ryan, noted:

> The bill under discussion has been advocated as a means of recovery from the industrial depression. . . . To advocate contraception as a method of bettering the condition of the poor and the unemployed is to divert the attention of the influential classes from the pursuit of social justice and to relieve them of all responsibility for our bad distribution and other social maladjustments.

While the other elites of the modern era may not have believed that free sex would usher in an earthly paradise, they all agreed that sexual "repression" was an unhealthy thing. A pivotal figure in this momentous cultural shift was, of course, Sigmund Freud, who taught that everything humans thought or did was ultimately motivated by sex. Others who believed in "free love" and dropping sexual inhibitions were George Bernard Shaw, H. G. Wells, and activist Mother Jones. It was all part of a revolution in culture that followed the First World War. Figures such as Albert Einstein, James Joyce, Marcel Proust, and various socialist revolutionaries sought to upend the old Victorian social and religious order.

The stories of these rebels have been well told—indeed, they are part of a sacramental cavalcade of progress venerated by liberals themselves—from Freud and the flappers, to the labor movements of the 1930s and 1940s, to Alfred Kinsey, to the beatniks, the hippies, and the AIDS activists of today. It's the long march of progress against the philistines of sexual atavism. Except that there really wasn't anything new about it—at least, in terms of its sexual philosophy. The sexual libertinism of the 1920s was just another revival of classical Gnosticism.

This is not as far-fetched as it sounds. In his book *Modern Times*, historian Paul Johnson explicitly called Freud a Gnostic: "He believed in the hidden structure of knowledge which, by using the techniques he was devising, could be discerned beneath the surface of things. The dream was his starting point." In his 1931 book *Old Errors and New Labels*, Fulton J. Sheen noted that the new humanism everyone was talking about was nothing but a revival of Pelagianism. This ancient heresy, founded by the monk Pelagius (354–420), denied the doctrine of original sin and held that humans could save themselves without the grace of God. "Humanism," wrote Sheen, "fails to take into account the sad lesson humanity had learned during the four thousand years previous to the incarnation; namely, that neither by his own human knowledge nor by his own human power is man able to make himself a perfect man even in the natural order. The two great peoples that divided the pre-incarnational world bear witness to this truth—the Jews and the Gentiles."

When George Bernard Shaw announced that discarding Victorian sexual reticence would cause a corresponding drop in lasciviousness—or "sex appeal"—he was met with disbelief by G. K. Chesterton: "There must have been hundreds of men in history, from pagan slave owners to anarchical art students who claimed that. There must have been all sorts of eastern despots in their harems and freak decadents in their hotels, who could do anything they liked in the way of decorum or indecorum, and have impropriety on as large a scale as they chose. Did it result in these cases in people becoming sexless, or insensible about sex or indifferent to sex appeal? Does it ever occur in any such cases?"

Chesterton would further observe, in an article called "The Moderns Rebel Against Modernism" that appeared in the *New York Times* in 1930, that many of those who were against the new sexual ethos were not prudes, but intellectuals—as well as the children of those free-thinking moderns. In a phenomenon that would be repeated in post-1960s America, when young conservatives rebelled against their libertine baby-boomer parents, children of the bright young things began to see their elders as, well, silly. Young people, Chesterton wrote, "are going back to something remote, as much as the pre-Raphaelites going back to the Middle Ages. In both cases the reason is the same: because the modern ages have become too unbearably stupid for intelligent people." He noted that both T. S. Eliot and Aldous Huxley—themselves hardly prudes— had grown tired of the bright young things. It is the intellectuals, Chesterton wrote, "who have now suddenly discovered the dangers of mere novelty, of mere anarchy, of mere negation." One writer broke new ground by starting every sentence with a lower-case letter. Chesterton saw this as a simple return to classic Latin form, and noted that the next groundbreaking step would have to be the elimination of letters themselves, which would result in a blank page.

One of Chesterton's contemporaries also saw the danger in the blank page, while at the same time trying to correct the Catholic Church's teaching on sex. His name was Dietrich von Hildebrand, and he was arguably the greatest lay Catholic of the twentieth century. Hildebrand was the son of a famous sculptor, Adolf, who created many of the fountains of Munich. Dietrich was raised in Florence, surrounded by art and atheism within his family. From a youthful early age, however, he felt the pull of Christianity and converted in the early 1920s.

In 1925, while he was a professor of philosophy at the University of Munich, von Hildebrand gave a series of lectures to the Federation of Catholic Students' Unions. The topic was chastity. Von Hildebrand reiterated Saint Augustine's three goods of marriage— *proles, fides,* and *sacramentum.* He then attempted to expand on them: "There exists, however, a profound relation of quality between the bodily union and that psychological and spiritual factor of specifically matrimonial love formulated under the terms *mutuum adutorium* (mutual assistance) and *fides* (fidelity) as one of three ends." What von Hildebrand was saying, in essence, is that sex was about more than procreation— "We should rather speak of the meaning of sex than of its function. . . . The act of wedded communion has indeed the object of propagation, but in addition the significance of a unique union of love."

Even if the intention to reproduce were invested with the noble purpose of giving the Church new souls, that intention by itself, to the exclusion of specific wedded love, could not organically unite physical sex with the heart and spirit, nor would it possess the power to inform from within the distinctive nature of sex, alloyed as it is by a tendency to overcome the spirit, and thus transform it into a positive good.

By "the tendency to overcome the spirit," von Hildebrand meant orgasm. "The spiritual person," he said, "is in danger of being 'swamped' by the orgasm." Sex involves "a flinging away of the self"—that is, "when it is not a divinely sanctioned surrender of self." When the divine purpose and function of sex is not present, von Hildebrand claimed, what can often surface is the ugly side of sex: "The moment the sexual act is not viewed from within, in its divinely ordained function, but appears in its external aspect, the stark vital brutality, the ugliness of certain features, makes itself powerfully felt."

Von Hildebrand would not be the only Catholic of the time to reassess the Church's strict views about sex in response to modern cultural conditions. In 1930, Rev. Felix M. Kirsch, a professor at Catholic University, published a book called *Sex Education and Training in Chastity*. Today, the title alone would be enough to elicit sarcasm and hostility from educators (even at Catholic schools). But Kirsch's book is wise. "The sense of modesty is one of the guardian angels given us by God for the safeguarding of chastity," he writes. Kirsch was no prude, however. He criticizes "exaggerated demands made in the interest of modesty." He rejects the claim made by one expert that letting young boys and girls acquaint themselves with their sexual organs "will surely lead to grave temptation during adolescence." Kirsch notes that there were Christian denominations which had even banned discussing the commandment against adultery for fear that talking about it would cause children to think about sex and thus be led into sin.

The alternative to this was not graphic sex education without morals; Kirsch warned against an approach to instruction that became "merely informational and . . . would reject moral education as a useless appendage." Kirsch called instead for a realistic approach that avoided "prurience and prudery." Christ himself spoke "naturalistically," saying in the Gospels that what comes from the heart out of the mouth is more important than what goes into the mouth, which "passes through." Kirsch quotes an Irish author who says of the Virgin Mary, she "spoke no prudery, for she knew no sin." Kirsch adds that Victorians (and even those living in the 1930s when the book was published) may have been scandalized by Elizabeth's salutation to Mary: "Blessed is the fruit of thy womb." (Kirsch was also prescient about our modern problem of declining birthrates in the Christian countries of the West: "Both old and young are seeking the pleasure of sex but are eliminating its creative power." He notes that the problem is particularly acute in France.)

Kirsch's colleague at Catholic University was psychologist Rudolf Allers. Born in 1883, Allers was a student in the last class taught by Freud at the University of Vienna. But he would eventually reject Freudianism, writing a book called *The Successful Error* debunking his former teacher. Allers came to the United States in 1938 and took a job at Catholic University. In 1940 he published *Character Education in Adolescence*. For Allers, sex was not about procreation, as the Church held for centuries, or about body parts, as the sex educators of the 1960s and after would hold. It was about the "longing for completion." This was a natural and spiritual completion to be found in true love, of which sex was only a part. Freud had found "all love being originally and basically sexual. The fact that no trace of sexuality may be found either in maternal love or in the love between friends, does not trouble the psychologist. Of course, adolescents feel strong sexual urges. But as they are just coming into realization of themselves as persons, there is an uncertainty, an anxiety and shyness."

This shyness is due partly to uncertainty in face of the new problems and the lack of self-reliance, and partly to the nature of sexuality itself, which is not simply a longing for union but contains, however dimly, the knowledge that union means, in a way, giving up one's self. Even in the crudest form of merely sexual desire, there is still a trace of this—that sexuality imports not only attaining satisfaction, but also giving something away.

How sweet this sounds, and how true, to ears that have spent a lifetime taking in the mechanistic, utilitarian messages of sex educators. They talk of condoms, disease, safe sex, and various erotic techniques, but lose sight of a core truth, perhaps *the* core truth: Sex involves giving something away, and that something is you. This irrevocable truth is why all the condoms and technical knowledge in the world won't take the fear, excitement, and pain out of sex. Or if they do, you wind up with Chesterton's blank page.

This was evident in 2006, when *Newsweek* produced another issue of *Current*, its college magazine. This issue was again preoccupied with sex. A large drawing made up half the contents page. It depicted a couple in bed. The woman is straddling the man, but she faces away from him and is reading a book. The man is sitting up tapping away at his laptop, which is resting on the woman's backside. She is—barely—clothed. He is faced with the female derriere and birth canal, and is entirely focused on the computer screen.

The cartoon is supposed to draw the reader in to the story that goes with it, about the abstinence movement on college campuses. It is intended, in fact, to emphasize the strangeness of abstinence. The article by Rebecca Rohr bolsters this position. Rohr interviews some kids wearing abstinence rings, then concludes that "with an estimated 75 percent rate of sexual activity, it may take more than a trinket and a pledge to accomplish this goal. For now, it seems, college students and sex are in a long-term relationship."

Presumably Rohr will have no trouble jumping from *Current* right to *Newsweek*. She has mastered liberal no-bias bias. These kids are trying to wait until marriage and abstinence may be the wave of the future, she reports. But statistics are statistics, and no "trinket" or dumb pledge is going to change that, she pragmatically concludes. What doesn't fit Rohr's thesis is ignored. The trauma of abortion, teen pregnancy rates, reports that the Pill kills sexual desire—all these pale beside the raw statistic that 75 percent of college kids are having sex.

Another piece appears a couple of pages later, on Fem-Sex, the new workshop given at Brown, Harvard, and Berkeley. It's a "safe space" for people "to explore their sexuality." All are welcome; students "use the term 'phe' instead of he and she." According to one facilitator, FemSex is "a sex-positive women's space." Hear, hear, says writer Alexandra Hiatt—a positive space, "and a stimulating one at that." So: abstinence, an impossible joke. FemSex, healthy and stimulating.

Yet *Current* may have accidentally stumbled across the truth even while trying to subvert it. When one first opens the magazine and finds oneself face-to-face with the drawing of the couple in bed too distracted to have sex, it's easy to think not of an abstinent couple who are so de-sexed that she can read and he can blog while their bodies are on top of each other, but of the Gnostics, who considered the body evil. The couple in the cartoon can have all the sex they want, yet it is sex without procreation, personality, heart, or laughter. One also thinks of those stories, now quite common, of men who cannot be aroused by a real living woman because their sexual gears have been stripped by pornography, which is the only thing that can stimulate them. Such is the triumph of modern sexual enlightenment.

Chapter Three

PHENOMENOLOGY

I N 1954, A YEAR AFTER THE FIRST ISSUE OF *PLAYBOY*
magazine was published by Hugh Hefner, Fr. Karol
Wojtyla, then a lecturer at the Jagiellonian University in Poland, completed his second doctoral thesis, *An
Evaluation of the Possibility of Constructing a Christian
Ethics on the Basis of the System of Max Scheler.* Scheler
had been a follower of phenomenology, a philosophy
founded by the German thinker Edmund Husserl. He
had also, in 1912, written a book called *Ressentiment.*
It explored the theory of what has come to be called
resentment, which Scheler explains as a self-defeating
hatred for something that one considers a barrier to
happiness. As thinkers like Albert Camus and John
Paul II would explain, resentment differs from anger
or rebellion in that it often attacks the good itself; one
doesn't hate a beautiful woman because she may be

conceited or arrogant, but simply for her beauty. It is a poison that would come into play in America after the sexual revolution.

Phenomenology as interpreted by the future John Paul II is a seemingly complex philosophical theory that can be understood and simplified by anyone who's been to a music concert. Let's take the rock band U2 as an example. The band plays their popular song "I Still Haven't Found What I'm Looking For." The song is about the spiritual quest for God and how it falls short of perfect realization on earth. While many in the audience realize this and sing along with understanding of the lyrics, each individual also brings his or her particular personality and life experiences to the interpretation. In the audience, for example, is a teenage girl who had an argument with her mother before the concert. When she sings the chorus—"I still haven't found what I'm looking for"—she thinks of her mother and how their relationship has changed since childhood. Standing next to her is a forty-year-old man who is contemplating a conversion to Catholicism. He has stopped drinking and taking drugs, and recently went to a mass. He still isn't sure what he will do. To him the song speaks to his spiritual crossroad. Next to him is a twenty-year-old drummer in a garage band. He loves the song's martial beat and jumps up and down in rhythm. These people all bring their subjective experiences to the objective values of beauty, truth, and faith represented in "I Still Haven't Found What I'm Looking For." Their individual responses reveal an objective reality. Phenomenology holds that people's subjective feeling, history, and experience are worth study and point to ultimate values and truth.

Wojtyla had discovered phenomenology when he was a student in Poland, which in 1954, when he finished his dissertation on Scheler, was occupied by Communists instead of Nazis. In the seminary, Wojtyla had absorbed the works of Aristotle and Thomas Aquinas, but felt that these older, objective philosophies took too broad a view of humanity, starting with a general theory of the universe and moving toward man. This left man as a creature without much freedom. Even more lacking was the dualistic and utilitarian philosophy of Bacon and Descartes, who held that man was the master of nature before the Fall and that was the state he was entitled (and intended) to recover; thus he could use material, including people, for his own satisfaction. Wojtyla would counter this view in his 1960 book *Love and Responsibility*: "Love consists of a commitment which limits one's freedom—it is a giving of the self. And to give oneself means just that: to limit one's freedom on behalf of another. Limitation of one's freedom might seem to be something negative and unpleasant, but love makes it a positive, joyful, and creative thing.

Freedom exists for the sake of love. . . . Man longs for love more than for freedom—freedom is the means and love the end."

In *The Theology of the Body*, John Paul II draws out the phenomenological meaning of the first three chapters of Genesis. He observes that there are two accounts of creation, the first an "objective" telling of God's creation of the universe and Adam and Eve in seven days. The second—which is actually the older account—describes the creation of Adam and then Eve. Delving into Adam's subjective experiences in the Garden of Eden, John Paul II notes that he was a person and not a man; in the ancient Hebrew, "Adam" simply meant mankind (or the clay from which humanity was fashioned). In Genesis, there is no distinction between male and female until after Adam awakes from his "deep sleep." It is then that Adam has the natural reaction to love—the desire to share it with another. The creation of Eve out of Adam's rib was therefore actually the creation of both man and woman. The fact that Eve came from a rib was not to give her lower status, but to emphasize that both persons were made from the same thing.

One of the disagreements that Wojtyla had with Scheler was that he did not see the reality of the human person's ability to self-consciously shape and create his own life. The theologian Fr. Richard Hogan uses the example of learning the piano to illustrate this point. Through self-awareness we can "watch ourselves" practicing the piano, and the experience thus becomes part of our consciousness. If I choose not to practice, I inadvertently shape myself into someone who is lousy at playing the piano. In Wojtyla's assessment, we "become what we do." We "determine ourselves," a reality found in the Genesis account of Adam naming the animals: "Man finds himself alone before God mainly to express, through a first self-definition, his own self-knowledge." Adam names the animals, thus becoming a creature who names animals—a person with cognitive ability. Adam has these experiences subjectively; it is what the future pope refers to as "original solitude."

Following original solitude comes "original unity"— when Eve was created. Before the Fall, sex was "a sacramental expression which corresponds to the communion of persons." It is a way to participate in the mystery of divine love. We participate by becoming, with our bodies, a sign of the divine love of the Trinity.

Wojtyla has offered an alternative to the idea that we reflect the Maker only as individuals. We imagine God "through the communion of persons which man and woman form right from the beginning." This constitutes perhaps the deepest theological aspect of all that can be said about man. And from this and from the beginning, "there descended the blessing of fertility." To turn away from this is to reject a blessing. The late pope believed that people have a memory or "echo" of what our bodies meant before the Fall. This explains why people instinctively cover up their bodies when naked. They are not so much ashamed or embarrassed by their bodies as they are instinctively protecting the body from lustful looks by others. This also explains Jesus' words that to even look at a woman with lust is to commit adultery in our heart. Wojtyla notes that Jesus does not specify whether the object of lust is the man's spouse or not. "Even if he looked this way at his wife, he could likewise commit adultery 'in his heart.'" Christ, it will be remembered, rebuked those who held to the Old Testament law that allowed for divorce. "It was not always so," Christ said. But because of "hardness of heart," mankind had forgotten the original nuptial meaning of our bodies and thus allowed for divorce.

Using a person for sexual self-gratification, even your own wife, rejects the total gift of self that sex is supposed to be. Of course, it is not easy to make a transition to a more pure vision of the sexuality of the human person. We must, Wojtyla writes, "be committed to a progressive education in self-control of the will, of the feelings, of the emotions: And this education must develop beginning with the most simple acts in which it is relatively easy to put the interior decision into practice." To not attempt this, to simply fall back into the cage of lust, is to live "in a state of continual and irreversible suspicion."

It would be decades before the mature thought

reflected in *The Theology of the Body* emerged into the popular consciousness. Furthermore, when Wojtyla was forming his ideas, Catholic schools had the reputation of being rigid and dogmatic factories of memorization and fear. To be sure, in many ways the Catholic Church before the cultural revolution was the sealed and repressive place it is often made out to be. There are no shortage of stories, from James Joyce to Mary Gordon to Edna O'Brien to John Powers, revealing Catholicism's hostility toward—even hatred of—sex. A large part of the problem was that the magnificent writings about sex by people like Dietrich von Hildebrand and G. K. Chesterton simply did not trickle down to the Catholic schools, which were often run by nuns and priests who taught the theology of the ruler. At the Catholic Education Week of 1942, one priest lamented that when Catholic school kids were forced to read Catholic authors, they emerged from the experience "as if coming back from a foreign country."

This was so despite the fact that there was a Catholic renaissance among intellectuals in the early- to mid-twentieth century—it produced converts such as Chesterton, Ronald Knox, Graham Greene, and Evelyn Waugh, as well as Jacques Maritain, Paul Claudel, Etienne Gilson, and Charles Péguy. Norway was home to Sigrid Undset, one of the great Catholic novelists of the twentieth century. But these artists were European;

in contrast to these lights were the American Catholic schools, which were often run by orthodox nuns and priests who taught dogmatic catechism. The Catholic-formed Legion of Decency censored movies for prurience. Heavily influenced by Thomas Aquinas and the scholastic tradition, many felt that, in the words of Catholic historian Patrick Allitt, "all the important questions had been answered." Books and articles on sex celebrated large families without much detail about the joy of the act that produces them.

One popular writer about sex and relationships before Vatican II was Monsignor George A. Kelly, who authored books like *The Young Catholic's Dating Guide* and *The Catholic Youth's Guide to Life and Love*. Kelly taught that the husband is the head of the household and that a woman degrades her noble calling by trying to have a career. The purpose of marriage and marital love was to have children. Yet Kelly also offered lessons that are perhaps more relevant than when he first offered them: "Love is not glamour." "Love is not an escape." "The three elements that masquerade as love— the lure of sex, the appeal of glamour, the promise of escape—probably are responsible for most marriages that hit the rocks."

Of course, the media focused more on Kelly's more old-fashioned ideas, leaving liberals—including liberals in the Church—struggling to appear more cosmopolitan. One group of Jesuits, desperate to foster a native Catholic literary culture, falsely claimed that British Catholic Theodore Maynard, who had moved to the States from Europe, was in fact American. Maynard himself was unambiguous about what he was facing: "Few Catholics are so badly instructed as those in this country," he wrote in the 1930s. Australian convert Frank Sheed started a publishing house, Sheed & Ward, but found it rough going. "The absence of a Catholic reading public was our continuing problem," he recalled.

In 1939, Pope Pius XI issued the encyclical *Divini Illius Magistri,* "On the Christian Education of Youth." Pius reiterated Augustine's three goods of marriage and in the section on sex education warned of the "very grave danger" of "naturalism which nowadays invades the field of education in that most delicate matter of purity of morals." Those who would simply teach a scientific, naturalistic version of sex ed "grievously err in refusing to recognize the inborn weakness of human nature." He then quotes the Christian writer Silvio Antonio: "Such is our misery and inclination to sin, that often in the very things considered to be remedies against sin, we find occasions for and inducements to sin itself." Therefore, Pius XI concluded, it is important that when a father discusses the facts of life with his son, he "should be well on his guard and not descend to details, not refer to the various ways in which this infernal hydra destroys with its poison so large a portion of the world; otherwise it may happen that instead of extinguishing this fire, he unwittingly stirs or kindles it in the simple and tender heart of the child."

Yet this fear of "naturalism" caused a dilemma: A naturalistic explanation of sex—such as was then being explored by Karol Wojtyla in Poland—itself reveals sex's holy and self-giving nature. That is to say, describing what happens physically during sex can produce not pornography, but sanctity. In "Contraception and Conjugal Love," published in 1961 in *Theological Studies*, Fr. Paul M. Quay, a brilliant Jesuit theologian and a physicist who graduated from MIT, wrote that Catholic theologians had for fifteen hundred years missed an essential truth about sex. For too many Catholics, the sexual act was intended solely for procreation, with the unity and love it fostered between the couple a secondary good. Quay called for a "third level of insight about sex," beyond a view based purely on pleasure and another based on procreation. He then offered this remarkable paragraph:

> The ultimate end of human sexuality is not carnal pleasure or companionship or marriage or children or the family or civil society, though it includes and requires all of these; for none of these is perfective of the person as such. The ultimate purpose of human sexuality, as of all else, is to raise the person and, through him, other persons,

to the most pure and exalted love of God. In so far as this can be achieved without sexual activity, sexual activity is unnecessary for a person.

Yet this was not cause for libertines and liberals to rejoice. Quay points out that this understanding of sex can only be fully understood through the prism of orthodoxy. Sex is about the love of God, a love that is fecund, bursting out and resulting in new life. Love by its nature expands and multiplies. Sex is about loving God, but that means loving God to the fullest—entering a divine love that creates life. Any attempt to block this love and its flowering results in reducing the other to an object—as Quay put it, a "reduction of the dignity of a human person to the status of a mere means to another person's wishes—the penultimate malice of all social sin."

Furthermore, marriage is not a license for unrestrained sex to be indulged in whenever the mood strikes. Indeed, restraint is necessary for the perfection of love. To Quay, "Marriage requires an ever-greater human control of coition and all that accompanies it, an ever-greater awareness of who one's partner is, and what one is seeking to say ever more perfectly to him or her by the word of love which is coitus." As Quay saw it, this "ever-deepening" spiritualization of the sexual act "may progress to the point where even at the moment of mutual orgasm, both are elevated in prayer, rejoicing in God for the gift of union He gives them, with each other and himself."

The sexual act, explained Quay, also has larger meaning outside the privacy of the couple. It reflects the union of Christ with the Church and the "eternally fruitful mutual love of the three persons" of the Trinity. The very body language of the lovers speaks to broader truths: the man's "penetration and permeation of her with his very substance"; how the woman "gives and surrenders herself to the man by complete openness, receptiveness, submission, and a full unfolding of herself"; to Quay, "the yielding of one's body to another is, thus, the natural symbol of willingness to become father or mother." It is a desire on the part of each lover to gain for the other "that exalted physical, mental, and spiritual maturity for one's partner which comes only from parenthood." This desire to impart virtue is present whether the couple is fertile or not.

Quay also drew a distinction between using contraception and using the rhythm method to prevent pregnancy. Contraception is a thwarting of the action of God in lovemaking, an action that can result in the profound grace of new life. The rhythm method calls for periods of abstaining between couples. These periods, according to Father Quay, can be seen as a form of penance—"a symbol of sorrow that children are not to issue from subsequent marital union; it is a sign of regret for the necessities imposing its practice." It is an acknowledgment of original sin and "stands for the submission of man to God in penitence and reparation."

As Father Quay noted, in the conjugal act the man and woman's actions toward each other reflect their desire and ability to be loving and caring parents—whether conception takes place or not. Their bodies reflect the language of parenthood, the self-giving and gentleness that it entails, even if children do not result.

In light of Father Quay, the theories of the sex liberationists seem not only silly, but inaccurate and extreme—and not just to conservatives. One of the most famous of the sex liberationists was, of course, Alfred Kinsey, whose sex report in the 1940s is considered a watershed moment in the sexual liberation of the Western world. Kinsey's strongest and most insightful critic wasn't some crabbed Elmer Gantry terrified of sex, but the brilliant literary critic and cold war liberal Lionel Trilling. In 1948 Trilling wrote a review of Kinsey's report, and his insights into Kinsey's *Sexual Behavior in the Human Male* are still valid. Trilling was no prude and no conservative. He opens his piece praising the Kinsey Report. "Nothing shows more clearly the extent to which modern society has atomized itself than the isolation in sexual ignorance which exists among us. We have censured the folk knowledge of the most primal things and have systematically dried up the social affections which might naturally seek to enlighten and release. . . . Probably our culture is unique in strictly isolating the individual in the fears that society has devised." Further, Trilling writes, "perhaps only science could effectively undertake the task of freeing sexuality from science itself. Nothing so much as science has reinforced the moralistic or religious prohibitions in regard to sexuality."

So far, nothing that today's high school sex-ed teacher wouldn't endorse. Then Trilling gets to the report itself. He notes that Americans—at least in 1948— had a slavish attitude toward science, and the report claims to be nothing other than scientific observations and data. And yet Trilling finds it "full of assumptions and conclusions; it makes very positive statements on highly debatable matters and editorializes very freely." The greatest flaw, according to Trilling, is "the question of whether the Report does not do harm by encouraging people in their commitment to mechanical attitudes toward life."

This mechanical attitude, of course, is what has triumphed today. Any dissent from the idea that more sex is always better—and that the more ubiquitous sex is in the media, the better and healthier for puritanical America—is quickly renounced in the name of health and science. Kinsey held that good sex means frequent and uninhibited sex. He wanted males to be able to match the ability of some animals to mate several times a day—"the more than daily rates which have been observed for some primate species could be matched by a large portion of the human population if sexual activity were unrestricted."

Trilling objects to Kinsey's report not solely on the basis of morality, but with common sense and even scientific observation that frequent sex can be a sign of anxiety and neurosis—"Adult intercourse may be the expression of anxiety; its frequency may not be so much robust as compulsive." Compulsive, or quick, behavior is not intrinsically better behavior for the individual or for society. "By such reasoning," Trilling writes, "the human male who is quick and intense in his leap to the lifeboat is natural and superior, however inconvenient and unfortunate his speed and intensity may be to the wife he leaves standing on the deck, as is also the man who makes a snap judgment, who bites his dentist's finger, who kicks the child who annoys him. . . ."

Trilling also nails Kinsey on his methodology. Kinsey did not use lie detectors in his tests. In such a test, Kinsey argued, "there is no way except to win voluntary cooperation through the establishment of that intangible thing known as rapport." According to Trilling: "It might be asked why a thing which is intangible but real enough to assure scientific accuracy should not be real enough to be considered as having an effect on sexual behavior." But such criticism did not come solely from fusty professors. The Kinsey Report also came under sarcastic review in the very first issue of *Play-*

boy. "Dr. Kinsey makes sex seem very, very serious," the magazine declared in the winter of 1953. "[*Playboy* cartoonist] Virgil Franklin Partch II just makes it funny as all hell—and personally, that's the way we prefer it." Even the libertine Hugh Hefner knew that sex was about more than plumbing.

As do we all. Shortly after I heard about Ellen's abortion in the late 1980s, I got a job working in a record store. I was finishing up my undergraduate studies at Catholic University and freelance writing, and I needed a steady supply of rent and food money. I had grown up with the Beatles, Van Morrison, Jimi Hendrix, and Bob Dylan—tastes I had acquired through my older brothers—and at the record store I experienced an even wider world of music. The store was in the city and was a picture of multiculturalism: African Americans, white prep school suburbanites (me), gays, hippies, stoners, jocks all worked there. I discovered black artists like Guy, Chaka Khan, and Bobby Brown, and gay favorites like the Pet Shop Boys and Bronski Beat. On weekends after closing the entire staff would go out dancing or to a concert. The rhythm united us, propelling us not toward Dionysian chaos (the drink and drugs did that) but a kind of one-family ecstasy. On many nights, sweating on a dance floor, I felt God. The movement of my body, which would have scandalized Miss Donahue and Sister Mary at Our Lady of Mercy, was a conduit to heaven. What was not was the promiscuity that had by then become a routine part of my life. The music industry was—is—full of alcohol, drugs, and late nights, but whereas the music would often lift me to God, my behavior often sent me crashing back to earth. As I said, these kinds of stories have become clichés in post-1960s America. It has become the dull norm, a dour, repetitive self-disrespect. It is the antipode to what the great priest Richard John Neuhaus called "the high adventure of orthodoxy."

What should be emphasized is that rock 'n' roll did not contribute to my promiscuity and resentment: It in fact offered a Christian alternative. It's amazing that popular music is still described as a harbinger of madness and antinomianism; I believe it has always been a form of prayer. There is a basic narrative of rock 'n' roll history proffered by *Rolling Stone*, MTV, and other liberal outlets. Once upon a time, the rock myth goes, America was an innocent, socially cohesive place where children were seen and not heard. Then in 1956, the sky cracked open, and down came Elvis Presley. Presley was sexual anarchy loosed upon the world, the prime mover in the forty-year rebellion against crushing middle-class values. According to *The Rough Guide to Rock*, a large book that advertises itself as a compendium of significant rock records, Elvis "appeared fully formed" from out of the earth. Defiantly wiggling his hips at staid, bourgeois America, he was "the first to present rock 'n' roll not as a dance party but as the soundtrack of alienated youth." This story is part of the gospel of the rock establishment and has been bought whole hog by conservatives; on page one of his jeremiad *Slouching Towards Gomorrah*, conservative hero Judge Robert Bork mentions Elvis along with James Dean and the Beats as "harbingers of a new culture that would shortly burst upon us and sweep us into a different country."

Yet if Elvis simply conjured the music he played out of whole cloth, then so did Sinatra. What Elvis played was simply his own version of jump blues, which had grown out of the swing that Elvis had grown up hearing in Memphis. If anything, Elvis was a product of the past, not a harbinger of the future. According to James Collier's *Jazz: The American Theme Song*, Elvis's music has its genesis in 1936, with a Chicago group called the Harlem Hamfats. The Hamfats were two brothers, Joe and Charles McCoy, who had grown up playing Mississippi blues. However, in 1936 swing was on the rise, and the McCoys's manager decided to bolster their sound by backing them with a hard-swinging New Orleans jazz band. The result was a hard-driving style that was so ebullient that soon other groups began playing "rhythm and blues" style, most famously Louis Jordan and His Tympany Five and Bill Haley of "Rock Around the Clock" fame. (Despite the *Rough Guide*'s assertion, this was, perhaps first and foremost, music for dancing.) From jump blues, it was just a small step to Elvis: "The line from the jazz-based music of the

Harlem Hamfats to Elvis Presley," writes Collier, "is astonishingly direct." This fact was verified by Elvis himself in 1956, when he mulled over why what he was doing was causing such a fuss: "The colored folks been singing it and playing it just like I'm doin' it now, man, for more years than I know. They played it like that in their shanties and their juke joints, and nobody paid no mind 'til I goosed it up."

Of course, there is no denying that Elvis caused rumblings in white racist America, which had an irrational fear of black music. Yet because the rednecks of the 1950s didn't appreciate rhythm and blues does not make those who reject Marilyn Manson similarly repressive or unenlightened. For one thing, even when Elvis was playing the most secular jump blues, there was a performance ethic that is completely foreign to many contemporary rock bands. Even when a blues musician was singing about lust, alcohol, and prison, there was a certain musical restraint in his playing, as well as a respect for the audience that seems almost quaint among rock stars today. Unlike sullen, sulky pop stars like Pearl Jam's Eddie Vedder, blues and jazz musicians played the hits to please the audience, craved popularity, and appreciated fame. B. B. King recently commented that it used to appall him when he saw young rock 'n' rollers smash their guitars. The guitar, said King, was the musician's "bread and butter," and destroying it was an act of profound contempt and stupidity.

There was another important similarity between Elvis and the musicians he imitated: the Christian Church. As Steve Turner notes in his absorbing *Hungry for Heaven: Rock 'n' Roll and the Search for Redemption,* Elvis, when growing up, had frequently visited East Trigg Baptist Church, where he saw Marion Williams, Mahalia Jackson, and other gospel greats. (Another regular visitor was a young boy named B. B. King.) Elvis himself was a member of the Pentecostal church, as was Jerry Lee Lewis. Other "pioneers" of early rock 'n' roll were also Christians: churchgoers. Chuck Berry, Buddy Holly, and Little Richard were Baptists. Of course, this doesn't mean that any of these men was the most pious member of the congregation or even that he went to church that frequently. Moreover, the secularization of gospel was often bitterly resented by gospel singers. Four months after Elvis recorded "That's All Right, Mama," Ray Charles recorded "I Got a Woman." By fusing the gospel song structure of the black Baptist church with secular lyrics, Charles crossed a barrier that left many in both the blues and gospel communities uncomfortable. Blues singer and preacher Big Bill Broonzy said, "He's mixing the blues with spirituals. I know that's wrong. He should be singing in church." The success of Charles led to a deluge of Baptists and Pentecostal blacks who parlayed their church experience to gain pop fame—Sam Cooke, Wilson Pickett, Aretha Franklin, James Brown, Lou Rawls.

Yet despite the frictions caused by the crossover artists, there has always been a tight connection between sacred and secular American popular music that stretches back to the first days of the Republic. The earliest immigrants to America brought their music traditions to the New World with them, whether they were New England Protestants singing British hymns, Irish Catholics enjoying Celtic folk songs, or slaves from Africa and the West Indies performing the polyrhythmic drumming remembered from their motherland. The place where these styles came together was New Orleans, the birthplace of jazz. At the time of the Louisiana Purchase in 1803, New Orleans was a city of 10,000—half black and half white. Having been owned by the Spanish and the French, the official religion was Catholic, but the black population practiced a hybrid of Catholicism and voodoo, which they had brought with them from Africa and Haiti. Indeed, many practitioners had icons of Catholic saints in their homes and often interchanged them with their African gods—thus, Legba, a god of the crossroads, luck, and fertility, easily was associated with Saint Anthony because in pictures both were depicted as old men in tattered clothes. Unlike the Protestant settlers who would arrive in New Orleans after the Louisiana Purchase, the Catholic leaders in the city did not prohibit drumming and dancing. According to Marshall Stearns, the founder of the Institute of Jazz Studies and the author of *The Story of Jazz*, when the steady rhythm of African drumming clashed with the European tradition of the marching band, jazz was formed.

While this was happening, another popular music form, the blues, was also being born, although the roots of the blues are more difficult to uncover than those of jazz. Blues historians have traced the form all the way back to the "griots" of Africa, men who served as musical storytellers for their community. As with jazz, blues formed when black and white musical styles met. Slaves who were brought to America adopted not only the language but also musical styles from the South, Appalachia, and Europe—not to mention European religions. As Richie Unterberger writes in *The All Music Guide to the Blues*, "gospel music afforded the African-American community opportunities to sing with committed fervor. The harmonies and solo vocal styles are still found in black music to this day, including the blues." Indeed, as blues historian Albert Murray points out in his seminal book *Stomping the Blues*, at times there was virtual osmosis between sacred and secular music: "In point of fact, traditionally the highest praise given a blues musician has been the declaration that he can make a dance hall rock and roll like a down-home church during revival time. But then many of the elements of blues music seem to have been derived from the down-home church in the first place."

So if the popular music of the 1950s wasn't quite

the revolution it's cracked up to be, when did the music change? How did we go from "Rock Around the Clock" to gangsta rap? One answer is provided by Martha Bayles, the author of *Hole in Our Soul: The Loss of Beauty and Meaning in American Popular Music*. According to Bayles, the Elvis phenomenon wasn't as much about American teenagers busting out of the hypocritical and unnatural constraints of their parents—although she does concede that Elvis represented an acceptable version of a black entertainer, and that this was groundbreaking for its time—as about dancing. By the time Elvis came along in the mid-1950s, the swing bands had been largely replaced by crooners like Bing Crosby, Perry Como, and Doris Day, and the kids wanted to dance. Any cursory examination of the experience of Elvis's first fans will reveal that none of them was interested in overturning social mores as much as they just wanted to have some fun on the dance floor.

Bayles also recaptures the Christian roots of rock 'n' roll from the modern rock academics. She dissects the work of Greil Marcus, the Berkeley professor who is one of the most respected wags in rock's critical establishment. In *Mystery Train*, his book on Elvis Presley, Marcus repeats the contemporary rock myth of Elvis as ur-rebel. He claims it was a "secret revolt against Puritanism that erupted in Elvis's hips, and sinfulness [that] brought [Elvis] to life." Elvis, apparently, represented the hope that joy and abandon can last "as Saturday fades into Monday." This is pure, anti-Christian hooey, as Bayles notes: "Typically, Marcus restructures the week so that Saturday fades into Monday instead of Sunday, the day when enthusiasm gets put to nonhedonistic uses. Ruled out of bounds is the possibility of an enthusiasm that subsumes or transcends the erotic." According to Bayles, the real shift in American popular music didn't come in the 1950s, with Elvis, but in the 1960s. It was in that decade, writes Bayles, that the positive, funny, sensual, and spiritual idioms of the African-American tradition collided with "perverse modernism."

Bayles defines perverse modernism as "the anti-art impulses of the European avant-garde, which gave rise historically to such movements as decadence at the end of the nineteenth century; futurism at the start of the twentieth; dada in the 1920s; surrealism and the theater of cruelty in the 1930s; and postwar retreads of these movements, such as happenings and performance art, in the 1950s and '60s." These influences came into rock 'n' roll when young Britons who were the products of that country's art schools began playing American roots music. The most famous practitioners were the Rolling Stones, who began as a third-rate blues cover band and quickly gained fame as the dirtier and more menacing alternative to the Beatles. According to Bayles, the Stones quickly gained fame through their rudeness to their own audience, iconoclastic behavior toward authority and bourgeois values, and Mick

Jagger's cross-dressing antics that are regarded as part of rock's grand tradition but in reality had nothing to do with the positive spirituality of American pop music forms.

Yet Bayles misses a couple of obvious points. First, rock and roll was—is—often expressive of perverse modernism lyrically, while being quite aesthetically beautiful sonically. Britney Spears's album *Blackout* is a masterpiece of dance music that was made while Spears was hitting a nadir of self-abuse (and one could argue that the album is a cry for heavenly intervention). And even while many of the bands of the 1960s were upending social mores, they were singing about love. They may have talked revolution, smoked pot, and driven limos into swimming pools, but again and again the theme of their music turned to matters of the heart. "Ruby Tuesday," "Let's Spend the Night Together," the weak blues of Led Zeppelin's first album— the bands sang as much about love as the crooners who had preceded them. But what about the rebellion of rock? What about "Street Fighting Man" and "Revolution"? Those are indeed songs of rebellion. But there is a crucial distinction to be made. They are songs of rebellion—not resentment. As John Paul II has explored in his examination of Max Scheler, rebellion and resentment are two different states of being. Rebellion is a fight for justice in an unjust world—a striving for the good. Resentment, on the other hand, is an attack on the good itself. In his book *The Rebel*, Camus marks the distinction, referring to resentment as an airless chamber of toxicity. This offers an image that applies to much modern pop music, particularly rap and heavy metal. Much of rap attacks the good itself, from the dignity of women to the virtues of prudence and temperance. The best pop music, on the other hand, explores human weakness and even jokes about falling short of the virtues—but never indicts the virtues themselves. The Irish genius Van Morrison offers a good example of the difference. In the last ten years no artist in pop has produced a body of work as vital and spiritually alive. According to the rock elite, Morrison is a dinosaur stranded on the fringes of pop. In reality, his music has more to do with rock 'n' roll's original ethos than anything topping the charts. Rock writer Steve Turner wrote a biography of Morrison, *Van Morrison: Too Late to Stop Now*, in which he recounts how Morrison grew up surrounded by American popular music. His father was a fanatical record collector and the Morrison home in Belfast was filled with the sounds of American jazz, blues, folk, and gospel, as well as the Celtic music and Protestant hymns of his homeland. Morrison claims to have experienced a feeling of "spiritual ecstasy" when he was a toddler and heard the gospel legend Mahalia Jackson on the phonograph. "It forged an indelible link in his mind between music and a sense of wonder," writes Turner. Morrison's 1994 live album *A Night in*

San Francisco is a breathtaking record, both for its musicianship and the spirituality that once fueled American pop music. When Morrison is performing "In the Garden," his paean to the wonders of nature, at one point the piano and bass get lighter and lighter, and the song seems to be ending. Then Morrison starts to sing: *"Sam Cooke is on the radio/And the night is filled with space/And your fingertips touch my face/Singing 'Darling, you send me.'"* Then, taking the cue, one of the backing singers begins to sing Cooke's "You Send Me."

It is a numinous moment. As most of today's rock fans undoubtedly don't realize, Cooke was the son of a Chicago preacher and a gospel singer before he started performing pop. It's as though Morrison intends to single-handedly put religion back into the center of pop, where it belongs and has always been.

I still remember the morning in 1989 when I was at the record store and a new shipment of the latest Madonna album, *Like a Prayer*, arrived. When I opened the box of new CDs, a familiar scent drifted up: sandalwood, often used in Catholic ceremonies. It was the scent of the Church. I was brought back to Our Lady of Mercy and Georgetown Prep, to the slow sensuality of the mass, the kiss with Lisa, slow dancing at a mixer, making love with Donna. Madonna had purposely added the scent, hoping that it would smell, according to her manager, "like the Sixties and like the Church."

At the time many Catholics called Madonna's scented

album the silly prank of a post-Catholic adolescent, but Madonna actually had something powerful and real to express. Her video for "Like a Prayer," the title track of the album, depicts a woman who witnesses a black man falsely accused of a crime. She hides in a church, prays to a statue of the black saint Martin de Porres, and falls asleep. In a dream the saint becomes her lover. Upon awakening, she realizes that with the power of God's love she can do the right thing. She fingers the real criminals and frees the falsely accused black man. Upon release, the video caused a major controversy. People thought Madonna was depicting Jesus as black and then making out with him; further, she was seen dancing in front of burning crosses. Liberals in the media defended Madonna as a martyr to free speech and delighted in her antics as a lapsed Catholic spitting in the eye of the Church. One Catholic bishop condemned the singer, and the conservative Catholic media reviled her as an attention-seeking prostitute.

Through all the smoke one clear voice emerged: the liberal priest Andrew Greeley. In a bitter and penetrating essay in *America* magazine, Greeley analyzed the video and was unsparing in his verdict. "Like a Prayer" was blasphemous "only for the prurient and the sick who come to the video determined to read their own twisted sexual hang-ups into it. Only for those who think that sexual passion is an inappropriate metaphor for divine passion (and are thus pretty hard on Hosea,

Jesus, Saint Paul, Saint Bernard of Clairvaux and Saint Teresa of Avila). Only for those whose subconscious racism is offended at the image of a black saint revealing God's love [is it offensive]." Greeley concluded that Catholicism "imposes on its children both obsessive and imprisoning guilt and a liberating sense of God's love as sacramentalized in creation and especially in human love. It is a paradox struggling to become a contradiction."

Greeley's article was published in 1989 and since then more people have come to know *The Theology of the Body.* So perhaps the paradox will not become a contradiction.

Chapter Four

THE NEW
COMSTOCKERY

"HAS THE CHURCH LOST ITS SOUL?" This was the question posed by *Newsweek* on October 4, 1971. In a lengthy story written by Kenneth Mann, the writer himself offered the answer: "The 'soul' of the U.S. Church—an integral Catholic subculture with its own distinctive blend of rituals and rules, mystery and manners—has vanished from the American scene."

A poll taken by *Newsweek* bore that out. Sixty-three percent of Catholics had not gone to confession within the previous eight weeks. Sixty percent did not think someone who divorced and remarried was committing a sin. Ninety-two percent could not name a decision made by the Conference of Catholic Bishops that had been important in their life. Seventy-three percent favored teaching sex education in schools—both Catholic and public. A third were against the Vietnam War and more than half thought priests should be able to get married. Fifty percent also thought it was fine to reject the Church teaching on contraception. Of all respondents, seventy-five percent were eighteen to thirty-five. And according to Mann, there was no holding back the liberal tide: "Both theologically and politically, conservatism has been reduced to a sectarian movement in American Catholicism, led largely by disgruntled converts devoted to the hopeless task of preserving the Church in a mold made by earlier generations. There are no compelling conservative minds in the Catholic press."

Perhaps Mann had never heard of Paul Quay, Rudolf Allers, Dietrich von Hildebrand, or even Jacques Maritain, a liberal who had expressed his doubt about the direction of the post–Vatican II Church in his book *The Peasant of the Garonne*. In 1969, von Hildebrand published a pamphlet: "The Encyclical Humanae Vitae—A Sign of Contradiction." Rather than being "devoted to the hopeless task of preserving the Church in a mold made by earlier generations," von Hildebrand took *Humanae Vitae* as an opportunity to make progress. In "A Sign of Contradiction," he noted that any talk of love between a man and a woman touched on "what used to be a kind of scandal in Catholic writings on marriage."

There was plenty of talk in the old Church about the will of the flesh, the "mutual help and assistance" conjugal activity could provide—"but one heard very little of love." He then offers this stunning passage:

It is shocking that in the past the real, valid motive for marriage has been for the most part overlooked, that the intrinsic relation of this type of love to a full mutual self-donation in bodily union has been ignored. Compared with this great, noble, and basic incentive, which the Canticle of Canticles says "is strong as death," the isolated desire of the flesh is superficial and secondary. Who can deny that it is this love which shakes the soul of man to its very depths, which marks the deepest experience in the natural realism of human life? Certainly, there is a broad scale in the potential of men for love, in the depth and completeness of love. Leonardo da Vinci said: "The greater the man, the deeper his love." Great loves, such as that between Leonore and Florestan in Beethoven's *Fidelio*, or St. Elisabeth of Hungary and her husband, or St. Louis of France and his wife, may be rare and presuppose great and deep personalities, but in every human being who has ever experienced a real love, limited and imperfect as it may be, it is the great, dynamic human experience in his life.

As if there were any doubt, von Hildebrand summed it up: "It cannot be stated with sufficient emphasis that the time has come for us to do away with the Gnostic and puritanical suspicion of spousal love—love in the most specific sense, of which the Canticle of Canticles speaks in such a unique way." Furthermore, we should read the Song of Songs "in its original literal sense; then we can breathe the atmosphere of this love, and see the sublimity of bodily union when experienced as the ultimate God-given mutual self-donation." It is in viewing it literally that we can finally grasp the use of it in the liturgy as an analogy of "the relation of the soul to God." There was a reason why scripture used sex and not friendship as the form of love analogous to our love for Christ.

To many Catholics, von Hildebrand was not relevant. The schism that split the Church had already occurred— at four thirty on Monday, July 29, 1968. On that day, Pope Paul VI issued *Humanae Vitae*, an encyclical which was supposed to settle once and for all the question about contraception and Catholics. In it the pope declared: "Every matrimonial act must remain open to the transmission of life. To destroy even only partially the significance of intercourse and its end is contradictory to the plan of God and to His will." It has become conventional wisdom that this was the moment when the Catholic Church split in two; there were countless Catholics, faithful and practicing, who used birth control, and *Humanae Vitae* would drive them out of the Church. This separated the Church into two factions: enlightened, progressive modern liberals who were products of Vatican II, the Church council of the early 1960s that liberals claim opened up the Church to the modern world, and constricted killjoys who hated sex and wanted to drag the Church back to the dark ages of the 1950s.

Yet this is a distorted picture. As we have seen, Margaret Sanger was not as much interested in true freedom as in sexual license and limiting the growth of the "inferior races." Like many modern liberals, Sanger would claim that the Church is an enemy of mankind itself. After *Casti Connubii*, the encyclical defending the position on birth control, was issued on December 31, 1930, Sanger responded:

> The Pope made it perfectly plain that Catholics are expected to give up health, happiness, and life itself while making every other conceivable sacrifice rather than to have dominion over nature's processes of procreation. His letter denies any claims of poverty, sickness, or other hindrances to proper rearing of children that are valid reasons for the scientific limitation of offspring. As for the breeding of criminal, diseased, feeble-minded, and insane classes, the Pope opposes every method of

control except that of suggesting to those unfortunate people to please not do it any more.

Sanger's position wouldn't get any traction in the
Church until the late 1960s. But what is striking is how
much of the Church's writing about sex before *Humanae Vitae* was beautiful and truthful. Before the opening of Vatican Council II in 1962, Catholic magazines
Commonweal and *Jubilee*—both progressive—asked
some important lay and religious people their views
on what they expected of the Council. Birth control
was hardly mentioned and no one asked that the doctrine forbidding it be changed. In the spring of 1965
Fr. Andrew Greeley wrote that American Catholics had
no problem with the Church teaching. Many Catholics
felt that contraception was an evil.

In 1962 a St. Louis pharmaceutical firm announced
that "a new push-button aerosol contraceptive foam"
was available and being advertised "in bridal, Negro,
and religious magazines, and in Negro newspapers."
The Jesuit magazine *America* editorialized in the form
of a conversation:

REPORTER: I hear that you're marketing a new
    aerosol product. Word is that it's foamy, like
    canned shaving lather or whipped cream. Any
    advertising?
PR MAN: There sure is. We've bought space in Negro

magazines, Negro newspapers and in some
religious publications. Bridal magazines, too!

REPORTER: That's limited coverage. Why so much of it
in the Negro press?

PR MAN: Just to get it started. When our product gets
a grip on the popular mind, we plan to spray the
whole country.

REPORTER: About those religious magazines. Any
names?

PR MAN: Later, not now. You can't tell about
reactions from some of these nuts with a fix on
the "dignity" of man, or whatever.

REPORTER: Let's get back to the Negro press.

PR MAN: You know how it is. Growing concern about
joblessness and the high cost of relief rolls. Our
product helps save you tax money. Cut down
on people, and you cut down on relief budgets!
Do you know that more than twenty-five percent of Puerto Rican wives have received our
product?

REPORTER: How? Across the counter?

PR MAN: Well, not exactly. We've had 1,400 people giving the stuff away all over Puerto Rico for four
years.

REPORTER: Just what does your product do? How does
it work?

PR MAN: Well, I suppose you could call it a kind of in-
secticide, depending on how you look at people.

In 1963, President Kennedy was asked about the idea of including birth control as part of foreign aid. Kennedy gave a vague answer about research into fertility. *America* again editorialized, dismissing "the trial balloons which are periodically sent up suggesting that the Church is about to change her doctrine on the immorality of artificial contraception. . . . The Church is not about to do any such thing." The editors continued:

> Another is that morality is not a magic incantation, by definition irrelevant to public policy. Marriage and the family are social institutions of fundamental public importance. People's beliefs about the nature and function of sex and marriage are moral beliefs. If the people who hold them also believe in God (and most people do), their moral beliefs are part of their religion. These beliefs cannot be ruled out, on that ground, from the discussion of public policy.
>
> All policies are framed ultimately in the light of some conception of human good. Those of us who believe that the practice of contraception is profoundly opposed to the true nature and meaning of marriage are not "seeking to impose our private beliefs on others" when we object to the fostering of contraception as a public policy. After all, the government is our government as much as any other citizens'. We have the same right and

duty as other citizens to support or oppose public policy in terms of what is good for human beings, as we see it.

What changed all this was not *Humanae Vitae* but the 1965 Supreme Court decision *Griswold v. Connecticut*, which ruled that all state laws banning the sale of contraceptives were unconstitutional. Such laws had been passed in Puritan America; but in 1948, when the issue came up in a referendum, it was the Catholic Church that had fought to uphold them. By the early 1960s, this had changed. Perhaps the best way of charting the progression of Catholic thought on the matter is through *Commonweal* and *America*, two of the oldest and most popular Catholic magazines of that time. Both, in 1963 and 1964 respectively, editorialized that laws prohibiting the sale of contraceptives would be overturned and that this was nothing to get overly excited about. But they still flip-flopped, often contradicting themselves.

In the winter of 1963, *Commonweal* columnist James O'Gara wrote, "The truth of the matter, I think, is that birth control is simply not a proper matter for public law, one way or the other. Good law demands a certain consensus, and that consensus is clearly lacking on this question." The marriage relationship, he concluded, is "personal and sacred. . . . We should keep the state strictly out of the bedroom." In 1964, *America*—which only months earlier had opposed government funding of birth control, claiming "it's our government too"— shifted positions. "It may be hard for many people to grasp," the magazine editorialized, "but the truth is that the state cannot effectively legislate against everything that is morally wrong. . . . When the community comes to be seriously divided over the morality of an action, the state's effort to prohibit the action by law becomes difficult and finally impossible." The Catholic magazines were in fact just catching up with the media, which had been running a campaign against the Church and its stance on contraception. In 1961, the popular magazine *Look* published an article by Fr. John A. O'Brien of Notre Dame. In "Let's Take Birth Control Out of Politics," Father O'Brien defended the Church's stance on birth control while arguing that the state should take no position on the matter. In 1963, Father O'Brien published the same article in two magazines, *Ave Maria* and the Protestant *Christian Century*, arguing for family planning and population control. Population control was the obsession of the increasingly hysterical media. At that point, however, much of the Catholic media wasn't giving way. In the Jesuit magazine *America*, John C. Knott refuted Father O'Brien: "The mind of the Church has been and is in favor of life. She is not frightened by the statistical data presented by demographers and described in nightmare terms by propagandists." *Commonweal* at this point started to flip-flop on the question of contraception, running both pro and anti pieces about the pill.

After *Griswold v. Connecticut* was decided, both *Commonweal* and *America* praised the decision—*America* even claimed that the court had discovered, in the right to privacy, a concept of natural law. Yet they did so with some reservation. In July 1965, William Ball, a Catholic New York lawyer, wrote a long analysis of the *Griswold* decision for *Commonweal*. Ball noted that the justices had found "emanations" and "penumbras" in the First, Third, Fifth, Fourteenth, and Ninth amendments in regards to a "zone of privacy" enjoyed by married couples. As Justice Arthur Goldberg wrote, "Although the Constitution does not speak in so many words of the right of privacy in marriage, I cannot believe that it offers these rights no protection." Ball agreed, but added a twist that today is revealed as prescient. He suggested that the ruling could get the state more, not less, involved in people's lives. "How far (apart from birth control) may the 'planning' in family planning be carried? Some may indeed see in these programs a sort of new Comstockery, with a now highly managerial paternalism towards the poor and often unspoken puritanical assumptions respecting 'undesirables'."

For its part, *America* magazine found it ironic that

in defending privacy, the court had gone past the Constitution and embraced natural law. Justice Hugo Black, dissenting in the *Griswold* case, said that the "penumbras" and "emanations" about privacy in the majority opinion were based on "natural justice." *America* noted the irony: "The court's majority appealed beyond the letter of the Constitution to a higher law. None of the Justices would admit it, but it does seem as if, in order to get rid of an anti-contraceptive statute, they had to appeal to natural law." At the same time, it was Catholics who argued against contraception on the grounds of natural law. The Supreme Court ruled that there was a natural right to privacy, even if not enumerated specifically in the Constitution or Declaration of Independence. Yet they found no such penumbra or emanation about the right to life, even if such a natural right is mentioned in the Declaration of Independence. But the real damage was to democracy itself. By overturning the contraception laws, the Supreme Court took decisions out of the hands of the people. Many commentators noted that the laws against contraception were not even enforced by the time of the decision. If the people of Massachusetts or Connecticut wanted the laws overturned, they could have passed it through the legislature. But what if the legislature passed a law requiring people to use contraception? This was the silly scenario presented by Justice Goldberg. In his concurring opinion in *Griswold,* Goldberg had found the right to privacy in "the traditions and collective conscience of our people." Yet the idea that having children is also a tradition, one that the American people support, according to Goldberg, was nowhere in the "traditions and collective conscience of our people." It's also in the natural law recognized in the Declaration of Independence. Free people given the chance to pass their own laws don't run a very high risk of passing laws calling for forced sterilization.

The ink was barely dry on *Griswold* when the federal government began to intensify its program of birth control. On October 21, 1965, the *Wall Street Journal* reported on the massive expansion of birth control programs. "It's the most startling reversal of federal policy I've ever seen," said one government official. The *Journal* reported that "for fear of encouraging promiscuity," some federal birth control programs had not distributed contraception to single or divorced women, even while others did. In the name of resolving this conflict, the Johnson Administration raised the budget of government agencies like the Children's Bureau and the Public Health Service. President Lyndon B. Johnson was careful not to publicize the changes. The *Journal* noted that he was intimidated by "northeastern Catholics." It's doubtful that Catholics would have revolted even if Johnson had announced the government's involvement in a prime time press conference. The years of propaganda, from John Rock's book *The Time Has Come* to the sarcastic articles in newspapers and magazines, and perhaps sheer exhaustion about birth control, took their toll.

Just a few weeks after he had approved the *Griswold* decision in *Commonweal*, William Ball testified to a Senate Committee against public funding of sex education. But it was too late. In both 1965 and in 1966, *America* magazine blasted the Church for its abject silence on government funding of birth control—funding, *America* often pointed out, that was aimed at reducing births in poor black communities. Then, on September 30, 1967, *America* published an editorial announcing that the number of Catholic doctors prescribing contraception was rising—and that the Church should follow the lead of those doctors. Suddenly, *America* had changed its view on contraception.

Conservatives were defending the Church's teachings on sex at a time when cultural forces far more powerful than the Vatican were shifting social mores. On October 22, 1975, Planned Parenthood issued a "five-year plan" whose preamble stated: "Universal reproductive freedom is a most essential step, if not the most essential step . . . to solve the most critical problems of hunger, deprivation, and the hopelessness of poverty, as well as the deterioration of our water,

land, and air." But there was more: The leaders of the
organization wanted to launch a campaign for "modi-
fying attitudes, behavior changes, and/or skills." They
wanted to "abolish the arbitrary and outmoded restrictions—legal, regulatory, and cultural—which continue
to limit the individual's freedom of choice in fertility
matters." It wasn't enough to offer abortions. The culture itself had to be changed—and it was already happening. The soft porn of *Playboy* had been replaced
by the brutal dehumanization of *Hustler.* Pornography
went from the Red Light District to Times Square. The
film *Deep Throat* sparked a controversy and changed
the way people viewed and consumed sex. According
to the documentary *Inside Deep Throat,* before the ex-
plosion of porn in the 1970s, oral sex was considered
inferior to normal sex—it was the province of prostitutes. After *Deep Throat,* oral sex went mainstream
and many of the most popular liberal films of the period were overtly misogynistic. *Dressed to Kill, MASH,*
and *Animal House,* to name just a few, treated women
as nags, sex receptacles, or ciphers. In 1979, historian
Christopher Lasch, who would convert to Catholicism
later in his life, published a surprise bestseller, *The Culture of Narcissism,* in which he argued that capitalism
and "the cult of togetherness" were destroying relationships between men and women. To Lasch, the capital-
istic "apotheosis of individualism" had changed the

"mode of making it—from Horatio Alger to the Happy Hooker." "Americans have not really become sociable and cooperative," he wrote: .

> They have merely become more adept at exploiting the conventions of interpersonal relations for their own benefit. Activities ostensibly undertaken purely for enjoyment often have the real object of doing others in. It is symptomatic of the underlying tenor of American life that vulgar terms for sexual intercourse also convey the sense of getting the better of someone, working him over, taking him on, imposing your will through guile, deception, or superior force.

Lasch also noted that there had arisen the demand that sex "satisfy all [our] emotional needs." Catholic writers had been pointing out the impossibility of this years before Lasch, and would years after; for the truth is that sex can never satisfy completely—only God can. This reality was startlingly described by Bishop Fulton Sheen in 1967:

> Despite even a mad pursuit of erotic pleasure, every pursuer runs up against two dead ends: first, he is never able to possess completely the person who is loved; the partner always remains an unassailable fortress, a closed garden, a heart with

its own thoughts and aspirations; second, even in the maddest pursuit of carnal ecstasy, the pursuer is always thrown back upon himself, alone and solitary. He started out to be a conqueror and he senses himself a victim. He plunges himself into an abyss where he hopes to be lost, but he floats again to the surface. He hopes to be absorbed in his new divinity, but like Baal, it falls apart. In fact, he is more lonely than before unless he accepts the other as a gift of God. Then joy reigns. Man is right in his pursuit of love; he is wrong in believing that the sparks he enjoys below have no flames from above.

Yet Sheen's type of priest was giving way to a newer, more libertine type. One of the most notorious taught at Catholic University, where I would be a student in the 1980s. His name was Fr. Charles Curran, and he was the man who would become the supernova of the Catholic Church and the modern upheaval over sex. Curran was born in 1934 in Rochester, New York, where at age thirteen he entered St. Andrew's Seminary. In 1955 he attended the North American College in Rome, a school for aspiring priests. Theology classes were taught, in Latin, at the nearby Gregorian University, run by Jesuits.

It was at the Gregorian that Curran met the German Jesuit Franz Hürth. Hürth taught theology and

it was widely believed that he had helped with or flat-
out ghostwritten many of Pope Pius XI's addresses,
pronouncements, and encyclicals, including 1930's
Casti Connubii, which condemned artificial contraception. (One Jesuit joked to Curran that Hürth "writes
occasionally under the name Pius XII.") One day, Curran approached Hürth greatly concerned about the
Church's position on a new invention called the Doyle
Cervical Spoon, which was intended to aid fertility.
Hürth was against use of the device, arguing that a
proper act of marital intercourse involved depositing
male semen in the female vagina, not into what Hürth
jokingly called a "Machinaum Americanam." However,
Hürth (and thus Pope Pius XII) was not going to con-
demn the spoon. It was "an American issue."

Curran was overjoyed. As he notes in his autobiog-
raphy, *Loyal Dissent*: "A few years later I came to the
conclusion that his [Hürth's] approach was a good
example of the problem of physicalism, whereby one
'absolutized' the physical act of marital intercourse."
While Curran was in Rome studying to be a priest in
the late 1950s, a quiet Catholic sexual revolution was
taking place in Poland, where a young priest named
Karol Wojtyla was working on a book about love and
sex. It was, its author claimed, a work that had been
"born of pastoral necessity." As a priest who had prepared young couples for marriage and heard plenty of
confessions, Wojtyla decided that the Church's sexual

philosophy needed to be explored with greater depth. The result of his vision, *Love and Responsibility*, was a revolutionary text. It presented the sexual act as something good and holy, refuting Augustine—and anticipating Paul Quay. It was published in Polish in 1960, a year before Quay's essay would appear.

Wojtyla separated sex into two categories, an "act of man" and a "human act." An act of man was based purely on instinct, while a human act contains a judgment about what is good, which in a healthy, moral person is a judgment for the happiness of the other person involved. For Wojtyla, sexual love is a beautiful and powerful example of the law of the gift—the law that holds that people do not become fully human until they freely give themselves. This gift of the self involves the entire person, which is why sex that does not take into account the well-being and personhood of the other person is sinful. Wojtyla wrote frankly about sex. Thus, if a man is to serve his wife well, he wrote, "it is necessary to insist that intercourse must not serve merely as a means of allowing [the man's] climax. . . . The man must take the difference between male and female reactions into account . . . so that climax may be reached by both . . . and as far as possible occur in both simultaneously." The man must do this "not for hedonistic, but for altruistic reasons."

Both Curran and Wojtyla had come to their very different conclusions based on pastoral experience, hours of hearing confessions, and dealing with the concerns of young Catholics. Curran, in short, believed in situational ethics. He felt that a couple could choose contraception or fertility aids if they had in mind another good—the ability to fully care for already-existing children, for example. Wojtyla believed that acts like contraception were always wrong. But there was a crucial difference: Curran misrepresented, or perhaps misunderstood, Wojtyla's philosophy. For the next forty years and up until the present day, Curran would accuse him of "physicalism," making absolute the physical act of sex without regard to external circumstances. This was a completely false reading. In *Love and Responsibility* and then *The Theology of the Body*, Wojtyla again and again emphasized that the sexual act was not good in and of itself, but became good depending on the intention of the participants. He quoted Aquinas: "The morality of the human act depends primarily and fundamentally on the 'object' rationally chosen by the deliberate will." Over and over the pope would teach that the morality of an act depended on the object of the acting person. For this reason, he explained, adultery could occur even during sex between a married couple, if the man begins to view his wife as an object of lust. This is hardly making absolute the act of sex.

Curran got a lot of his ideas while in Rome, when he came under the influence of liberal theologians. Priests like Josef Fuchs and Bernard Haring (two Germans) opposed the "classicist" view of moral theology, which (according to historian Larry Witham) held "that moral action can be deduced from fixed, static natural laws that exist apart from history and persons and make certain actions always wrong." This approach made morality something of a science. The priest was to use fixed rules to determine the sin and prescribe the proper penalty and penance. Fuchs and Haring believed in subjective morality instead of absolute norms—one's history and situation played a part in the seriousness of a sin.

In 1959, a year after the conservative Pope Pius XII died and was replaced by Pope John Paul XXIII, who would convene Vatican II, Curran, then twenty-five, came under the tutelage of Haring. In 1961 he returned to Rochester and took a job teaching at St. Bernard's seminary. He didn't last very long. The Auxiliary Bishop of Rochester felt that Curran was too heavily influenced by "the German theology." But Curran's views soon brought him to the attention of the academic and political elite. In 1963, he presented a paper on Catholic moral theology at Harvard. It's important to remember that this was all around the time of Fr. Paul Quay's revolutionary article on the meaning of sex in theological studies. Quay's article, which surpassed *Humanae Vitae* for wisdom, depth, and pure poetry, came and went as did its central, obvious point that the reason for sex was to elevate another in praise of God and not necessarily to have children.

Curran was too hot for St. Bernard's, which was nicknamed "the rock" for its conservatism, and in 1963 he was offered jobs at Catholic University and Notre Dame. He was ultimately hired by Rev. Walter Schmitz, the head of the theology department at Catholic University. In the fall of 1964, Curran came out officially against the Church's position on birth control and in 1965, at a public talk to priests, he again declared his opposition to the ban on contraception. It was around this time that Curran came to the attention of Hugo Maria Kellner, a New York doctor and orthodox Catholic. Kellner was appalled by Curran, and wrote letters to the Bishop of Rochester complaining about the young priest. In one missive he expressed offense at "the unrestrained language [Curran] used in his lecture, [which] seems to indicate that Father Curran's imagination is unduly preoccupied with the sphere of sex." Indeed, at Catholic University, Curran taught an entire graduate seminar on masturbation.

Curran was both highly intelligent and a master of evasion. Something of a con man, he made the authorities at Catholic University look like doddering saps. In September 1966, the *National Catholic Reporter* ran an article about him based on lectures he had given and also a phone interview. In the piece, Curran predicted the end of the Church's authoritarian moral teachings; future morality would be based on "the experience of Christian people." Then this: "We today are beginning to break away from absolutism; and this is precisely where the risk, the danger, the insecurity, the name-calling starts coming." When Curran was questioned about the article, he replied that it was "somewhat inaccurate." The *National Catholic Reporter* ran a response defending itself, adding that Curran had been given the article to read before publication and had even made changes himself. When the vice rector of CUA demanded an explanation, Curran advised him to read all of his previously published articles to understand their "nuance." The dean apparently demurred. However, Fr. Francis Connell, the former dean of theology at CUA, did read Curran's 1966 book *Christian Morality Today.* He was not impressed:

> It is incredible that a book like this could be published by a Catholic priest, especially one who holds the important function of a teacher in the Chief Pontifical University of America. It is filled with errors. Unless something is done soon by ecclesiastical authority to remedy this situation, great harm will be done to the Church.

For most of its history, Catholic University had been a docile campus run by conservative clerics. Students and faculty followed the mainstream and the board of trustees. Liberals who in 1905 supported "Americanism"—openness to democracy and religious tolerance—were driven from campus. When Bishop William J. McDonald was made rector in 1958, he warned against modernism, telling the students not to be "dazzled by the claims of the so-called enlightenment and of the other more recent movements and philosophies which promised to be harbingers of a bright new world." In 1962, the first year of Vatican II, McDonald prohibited the Canon Law Department of the university from sending suggestions to the council. In 1963, McDonald cancelled lectures by Church liberals John Courtney Murray and Hans Küng. He also cancelled a symposium on Darwinism. In 1963, McDonald also dismissed Rev. Edward McBrian, a liberal, from the school of theology. The faculty of the school objected in a letter but didn't follow up with anything stronger. The campus newspaper, *The Tower*, barely commented on the firings.

Yet in four years, things had changed. Many of the students who came to Catholic University in the next few years were children of Vatican II, which ran from 1962 to 1965. They had also been inspired by the Civil Rights Movement and the bourgeoning rock music, free speech, and antiwar movements. (Among their number was Susan Sarandon, who would enter Catholic University in the early 1960s before going on to a Hollywood career and a lifetime of liberal activism.) These were kids profoundly affected by pop culture and the media—and the media in the 1960s had grown increasingly hysterical, unreliable, and hostile to Catholicism.

While Bishop Sheen and G. K. Chesterton had once been media celebrities, the press now elevated Church critics. In 1963, *Newsweek* characterized the Church's position as "blindly archaic," even if there were signs that it was becoming more "modern." The media also tended to give prime space to dissenters on contraception and ignored defenders of orthodoxy. Notre Dame's Fr. John A. O'Brien was featured on the front page of the *New York Times* after he wrote several articles about family planning and asked for a White House conference on population control. *Newsweek* quoted members of Planned Parenthood saying that Father O'Brien's views were "a source of joy." Front-page coverage was given to a Notre Dame conference, funded by the liberal Ford Foundation, that aimed at changing Church teaching. Books like *What Modern Catholics Think About Birth Control* and *Contraception and Holiness* got major play in the media, while conservatives were ignored. One of the biggest media darlings of the time was Dr. John Rock, who in 1963 published *The Time Has Come: A Catholic Doctor's Proposals to End the Battle Over Birth Control*, in which he advocated that the Church change its position on birth control. The book was excerpted in the *Saturday Evening Post* and *Reader's Digest*. The *New York Times* featured Rock on the front page. In one article, Rock said that the problem of overpopulation was so dire that Catholics should simply ignore Church teaching. "They can't take my Church away from me," he said. "I'm in this fight for good." Like Curran, Rock was a media-savvy character who could change positions depending on the audience. In 1966, he said he would never prescribe abortifacients. In 1973, he had become the "Father of the Pill" and rejected Church teaching on abortion.

Much of this was fueled by one of the biggest causes of the day: the so-called population crisis. On radio, television, and in countless magazines and newspaper articles, a prophet warned of the inevitable catastrophe if population growth was not curbed. The coverage, as historian James Hitchcock noted, "was urgent, panicky, and sometimes bordering on the dictatorial." The faculty at Catholic University had also become more liberal in the Vatican II years. In the School of Theology, conservatives Joseph Fenton and Rev. Francis Connell left in the mid-1960s, and the new dean, Rev. Walter Schmitz, hired liberals, including Father Curran. It's important to note, however, that many of the liberals of the 1960s were not of the new left, a much more radical wing of American politics. Dissident theologians who had been barred from Catholic University's campus, like John Courtney Murray and Hans Küng, were often faithful to the Church in ways that today would be considered conservative. Thus in 1964, *America*, the liberal Jesuit magazine, rebuked those who thought Vatican II would bring an end to the ban on contraception. The buzzword at the time was "aggiornamento," an Italian word meaning "to modernize and bring up to date." The Church, opined *America*, would "disappoint those who think that aggiornamento is the Italian word for contraception."

It is important to note this, because for many of those who would protest the dismissal of Father Curran, the issue wasn't contraception: It was academic freedom. A year before Curran was dismissed, the campus was the site of a small protest against Rector McDonald's unilateral decision to move the undergraduate Religion Department, which had been in the School of Arts and Sciences, into the Theology Department. It was a move intended to ensure that McDonald could have more control over what was taught in the undergrad Religion Department. Small groups of protesters popped up around campus, but their numbers were too small to win the day. This would change, as would the nature of American liberal Catholicism, when Catholic University attempted to let go Father Curran. When the news of Curran's firing arrived, years of pent-up anger at the iron rule of McDonald and other conservatives erupted on campus. Yet many of the protesters would be moderate faculty members and students who were fighting for academic freedom more than sexual license; one eyewitness wrote in *Commonweal* that there were no wild, irresponsible demands, and that the leaders even encouraged the student protesters to dress properly.

The day after Curran's firing, the theology faculty sent telegrams to the university trustees and organized a press conference for the next day. The students formed a steering committee, which claimed that with the Curran dismissal, "there has been a serious violation of academic freedom, of Christian justice, and the spirit of the Second Vatican Council." After all, Vatican II had declared that "respect and love ought to be extended also to those who think or act differently than we do in social, political, and even religious matters. In fact, the more deeply we come to understand their ways of thinking through such courtesy and love, the more easily we will be able to enter into dialogue with them."

The Curran affair broke right after 1966, the year after Vatican II ended and a pivotal year in the culture of the Church. It was here that resentment began to creep into mainstream liberalism. While the Second Vatican Council had allowed for some small changes in the Mass—while still allowing for Latin, Gregorian chant, and the veneration of saints—progressive activists called into question the legitimacy of the Mass itself. During the 1966 liturgical conference in Houston, reports surfaced of unorthodox "Masses" being conducted in the hotel rooms. That same year Colman Grabert, a Benedictine monk, suggested that the Mass should have "the fun of a successful cocktail party." Jesuit John Allen called the Mass a breeding ground for atheism because it separated man from God. Popular Catholic writer Mary Perkins Ryan called the Mass archaic and irrelevant. All of this was on the heels of the 1965 book *The Secular City* by Harvey Cox, which claimed that modern man was secular and uninterested in "ultimate reality."

This was all a shift from classical liberalism. As James Hitchcock has noted, "The complacently pragmatic and optimistic spirit of the New Frontier began to give way to more frequent and more obvious manifestations of angst, identity problems, and the search for meaning, all of which seemed to lead away from pragmatism and politics and back into the soul, to the spiritual life, to metaphysics, even to ritual."

The fight over Charles Curran would be waged by mostly calm liberals and the old conservative guard— but out of the crisis there would emerge a new, angry young left in the student body, the priesthood, and the media that was as dictatorial and narrow-minded as McDonald had ever been. The day after Curran's firing, the Theology Department, led by Professor Schmitz, who had hired him, came to the professor's defense. Schmitz noted that Curran's orthodoxy had not been challenged. This key component, a grave mistake by McDonald and his supporters, had left an opening for the protesters. If Curran's orthodoxy was not in question, then he was being railroaded without due process. *Humanae Vitae*, the encyclical upholding the ban on contraception, was a year away. By concentrating simply on the issue of due process, Schmitz was able to win over all the other departments with the exception of the School of Education.

At first, the faculty attempted a private reconciliation with the trustees and bishops. They sent out telegrams expressing concern over the firing. The trustees, old-school conservative Catholics who found it unprecedented to be challenged by junior clergy and faculty, refused to answer. Two days later a boycott was called. Classes were empty and the campus filled with thousands of demonstrators. Students gathered and at one point they substituted "cardinals and bishops" for "senators and congressmen" in Bob Dylan's "The Times They Are A-Changin'." Predictably, the media fawned over Curran. News teams gathered to cover the action, rarely, if ever, interviewing those in favor of his firing. The *New York Times* took note of the fact that Curran drove a car without a muffler and was called "Charlie." For a penance, Curran had two women bake cakes for their husbands. According to many on campus, he was "one of the greatest Christians" at Catholic University. Yet for all this praise, Curran's followers were not enthusiastic about encouraging people to hear his lectures. The *National Catholic Reporter* put it this way:

> Admirers spoke of [Curran] as one of the brightest young American theologians around, but dis-

couraged publicity about his talks. "Take it easy on Charlie; we need him" was the response of one priest asked by a newsman for tapes of some Curran talks.

It's worth noting this change in the media, as it would affect coverage of religion and sex up to the present day. Those hostile to the Church were transforming from liberals with a sense of immutable values to resenters out to attack the good for their own satisfaction and pleasure. The philosopher Irving Kristol once noted that in order to become a conservative in the 1960s, one had simply to stand still. Liberals were attacked viciously not so much from the right as from the new left, whose attitudes increasingly infected the media, erecting a new Comstockery—which is another term for punitive liberalism. Like the old Comstockery, the new Comstockery used censorship to silence those it disagreed with—or rather, it used silence. Chesterton, Dietrich von Hildebrand, Rudolf Allers—these were forgotten giants, men whom even the Catholic University students didn't recognize.

To be sure, there had always been media hostility toward the Church, but there had also been a willingness to engage with the orthodox—to allow their opinions, and even celebrate them, as well as to debunk nonsense on its own side. One of G. K. Chesterton's first adversaries was Robert Blatchford, a British socialist who started his own paper, *The Clarion,* in 1891. Blatchford wanted to put his ideas up against the best of the other side. He therefore turned the pages of *The Clarion* over to Chesterton in a debate that went on for months. Chesterton's other jousting opponents included George Bernard Shaw, Clarence Darrow, and H. G. Wells. In 1931, a writer for the *Nation* watched Darrow get crushed in a debate with Chesterton. The liberal icon was so inept, the writer noted, that Chesterton himself was disappointed: "Mr. Chesterton wasn't getting his exercise." Likewise, when Alfred Kinsey published his report on human sexuality in the 1950s, his major dismantling came at the hands of liberal Lionel Trilling. Beatnik Jack Kerouac once upbraided his friend, the radical Allen Ginsberg, for disrespecting the flag. The '60s changed all this.

In the end, Father Curran won his battle with Catholic University—at least for a few years. A week after being dismissed he was reinstated, made an assistant professor, and given tenure. The fact that Curran's orthodoxy was not questioned was the loophole that allowed him to be reinstated. Several bishops came to the defense of academic freedom. On April 26, 1967, Rector McDonald called a press conference to announce that they had rescinded their action in letting Curran's contract expire. Archbishop Patrick O'Boyle of Washington was quick to attempt a clarification: Anything involving the Curran case "must not be interpreted as in any way affecting the theological issues injected by the news media. In particular, this decision in no way derogates from the teaching of the Church and statements by the Popes and Bishops on birth control."

There was, however, one real casualty of the Curran affair. Msgr. Eugene Kevane, an orthodox priest and the dean of the Catholic University School of Education, had defended the bishops, writing that "the embodiment of knowledge and wisdom on religious matters is not to be found in the group of scholars and specialists in the sacred science, but rather in the successors to the apostles." As a result, Kevane was accused by the Department of Theology of libel. At meetings of the Education Department young radical priests who supported Curran were disruptive and even attempted to delay Kevane from grading papers on time so that students would consider him incompetent. One witness, Sister Mary Verone, who had taught at Catholic University since 1939, wrote that Monsignor Kevane "is literally enduring a persecution and a martyrdom." A reporter for the Catholic News Service noted the obvious irony: Professors at Catholic University were willing to tolerate dissent by Charles Curran, but when Kevane dissented from their dissent, the same professors "were not able to be equally indulgent."

Despite being reelected as dean in 1967—employing what one witness called "highly unethical and irregular procedures [that] were used to apparently intimidate certain faculty members prior to the election"—Kevane was canned in February 1968. The school rector, John Whalen, said that the faculty of the School of Education was divided about Kevane, "with no strength of leadership in between."

Monsignor Kevane decamped for another school and was forgotten. There were no editorials about his dismissal in *America* and *Commonweal*, which had both loudly supported Father Curran. The *New York Times* was silent. Kevane himself never named the priests who had been harassing him and they remain unknown to this day. He didn't write or speak about the episode—at least not directly. In December 1973 Kevane wrote an article on the Apostles' Creed, the most fundamental proclamation of the Catholic faith. Kevane noted that there were those who were brandishing a new Christianity that was pliable to modern history and culture. When the traditional Church reacted negatively, the dissenters "blessed the conflict, declaring that out of it a new synthesis would arise and hoping for a church-of-the-future, for a re-interpretation of adapted doctrine, which will harmonize better with what are called contemporary historical conditions, which will make religion more successful in winning modern man, and which will even generate that spiritual unification of mankind for which modern man recognizes so great a need. The synthesis sounds so good, and forward-looking, that many give up the faith for it." Those who resisted were suddenly known as conservatives. "As this strategy of politicizing our holy Religion proceeds," Kevane concluded, "men become ashamed to wear the tags and the labels which have been attached—to what?—of all things, to the very truth of God."

Still, despite his victory in the 1967 strike, Curran had remained under scrutiny by the Vatican. His file— number 4866, the last two numbers indicating the year it had been started—was still being added to. In 1977, the Fellowship of Catholic Scholars, a conservative organization, was formed and many theologians were openly challenging and denouncing Curran. In February 1979, Curran was scheduled to give a talk on Christian social ethics at Louisiana State University. Baton Rouge Bishop Joseph V. Sullivan cancelled the event after *The Wanderer*, a conservative Catholic newspaper, sent him a list of eye-opening quotes from Curran's books, articles, and lectures.

By this time many new Comstockers in the Catholic Church had taken over catechism and sex education. One series of educational books, called "Becoming a Person," caused an uproar among what were now known as "traditional" or "orthodox" Catholics—the same people who a decade earlier had simply been called Catholics. "Becoming a Person" was heavy on charts, graphs, and diagrams that explained the nuts and bolts of sex, leading one Catholic to dub the series "Becoming a Plumber." "Becoming a Person" was discarded, only to be replaced by the *New Creation* series, which also caused problems for its explicit nature and lack of references to Catholic doctrine. In many of the public schools, Planned Parenthood was writing the curriculum. In 1975, the Vatican's Sacred Congregation for the Doctrine of the Faith issued its "Declaration on Certain Questions Regarding Sexual Ethics." The Declaration reiterated Church teaching—and completely lacked the wit, wisdom, and earthy sensuality of Dietrich von Hildebrand, Chesterton, and Paul Quay. It spoke of "the present period" and its "corruption of morals," the result of "man's innate weakness following original sin; but it is also linked with the loss of a sense of God, with the corruption of morals engendered by the commercialization of vice, with the unrestrained licentiousness of so many public entertainments and publications, as well as with the neglect of modesty, which is the guardian of chastity." All true, but it would be hard to imagine a more dry recitation of church doctrine.

Luckily the counterrevolution was about to arrive. It began on September 5, 1979, the day John Paul II conducted the first of a series of general audience addresses about the nature of human sexuality and love. Together they would become known as *The Theology of the Body*. A year later, in the fall of 1980, the Jesuit magazine *America* devoted several pages to *The The-*

ology of the Body. Theologian Mary G. Durkin noted that while "Pope John Paul II is often regarded as a conservative theologian . . . his view of sexuality, though based on tradition, is revolutionary." Durkin observed that the pope's call to remember the echo of our lives before the Fall—our original solitude, original nakedness, and original innocence—and to celebrate sex and treat people as persons and not objects would be rejected both by old conservatives in the Church and the narcissistic liberal New Agers. Durkin then cited a favorite passage:

> We need to celebrate human sexuality because through it we discover the meaning of life. It is part of our nature to realize that we are "alone" and in constant search for our identity. Because of our loneliness we discover the real meaning of our existence when we assume as our own some of the "loneliness" of our partner in the act of sexual intercourse. Through physical nakedness we discover that man and woman are two different ways of being a human and thus come to an understanding of the importance of unselfish giving of ourselves as we become one but remain two individuals. The love needed for truly unselfish giving is a model for all true human communication. When a man discovers the femininity of a

woman and she the masculinity of him, they both
arrive at a deeper appreciation of the meaning of
their lives.

In June 1979, Curran had received a letter from
the Vatican. The Congregation for the Doctrine of the
Faith had "judged it necessary to examine" some of his
works. This was on the heels of several articles that
claimed that, contra Curran and the liberal theologians,
Humanae Vitae was indeed an infallible teaching. One
of the most brilliant proponents of this position was
William May, a professor at Catholic University. May
had originally been one of the signers of the 1967
petition defending Curran, but shortly afterward he
changed his mind. May would deeply regret his defense of Curran, even though he liked Curran personally. He would call Curran "a friend, a good man . . . a
good Catholic, in many ways a holy man . . . but I
think he is wrong." May insisted that the Magisterium of the Catholic Church, made up of the pope and
the bishops, thought infallibly, at least under certain
conditions. May—and other orthodox writers—often
quoted this passage from *Lumen Gentium*, a document
of Vatican II: "Although the bishops, taken individu-
ally, do not enjoy the privilege of infallibility, they do,
however, proclaim infallibly the doctrine of Christ on
the following conditions: namely, when, even though

dispersed throughout the world but preserving for all that amongst themselves and with Peter's successor the bond of communion, in their authoritative teaching concerning matters of faith and morals, they are in agreement that a particular teaching is to be held definitively and absolutely" (*Lumen Gentium*, no. 25).

May and others—most notably Cardinal Joseph Ratzinger, who would go on to become Pope Benedict XVI—made the point that Christ had promised to guide us in moral matters and that the Holy Spirit would prevent the Church from falling into error. May noted that while the bishops' teaching against the first use of nuclear weapons was one that a Catholic in conscience could dissent from, particulars about war, such as the killing of innocent civilians were "not absolutely binding." Pope John Paul II, when asked directly about Curran, answered that the Ten Commandments and Christ's commandment to love one another were never declared infallible teachings by the Church. The point of having a conscience, defenders of *Humanae Vitae* said, was to have a conscience "rightly ordered" to the truth. In 1985, the Vatican asked Curran to recant his positions: "The positions you have maintained on various important elements of moral doctrine are in open contrast with the teachings of the Magisterium. The Congregation now invites you to reconsider and retreat those positions which violate the conditions necessary for a professor to be called a Catholic theologian." In a meeting with Curran, Archbishop James Hickey told him that this was "a solemn warning." Curran had tenure, yes, but as a professor at Catholic University, he also had a canonical mission to teach matters of faith and morals. And that mission could be withdrawn.

Curran offered a compromise. He would stop teaching sexual ethics, the Vatican could list his errors, but he would remain "a Catholic theologian in good standing." This wasn't good enough for Rome. In March 1986, Curran traveled to the Vatican to meet with Joseph Ratzinger, the prefect of the Congregation for the Doctrine of the Faith, the Vatican office charged with enforcing orthodoxy. His compromise was rejected. Curran returned to Washington, D.C., and held a press conference. "I cannot and do not retreat," he said. "I have never been told who my accusers are." Ratzinger was having none of it: "Your own words have been your accusers," he wrote. Curran was dismissed. He took his case to court and lost.

Unlike the 1960s, the campus didn't seem to care very much about the Curran controversy. Ironically, the triumph of Curran's ideas had undermined his support. The students had grown up during the sexual revolution. To them, the war was over. They had premarital sex and used contraception. The student newspaper *The Tower* editorialized against Curran, then nine months later supported him. In yet another editorial, they cursed both sides—"one also perceives a vast number of those who could care less while Conservatives battle Liberals." This the harvest of twenty years of dissent—dissent which was written into Catholic school curriculums and textbooks—and the fruit of the sexual revolution. Sex, drinking, and parties were more common at Catholic University than chastity and prayer. After all, these were kids—my generation—who had grown up at folk Masses and reading books like the "Becoming a Person" or the *New Creation* series, which was published in the 1980s. The *New Creation* books were heavy on sex, going so far as to reject the idea that children had a latency period. In describing the Annunciation, there was no mention of Mary's virginity. It was years of this kind of bad catechism that laid the groundwork for the widespread apathy among Catholics that met the firing of Charles Curran in 1986.

On June 25, 1986, Curran received a letter from Joseph Ratzinger—Curran was neither "suitable nor eligible to exercise the function of a professor of Catholic theology." On August 18, Curran came to the residence of Archbishop Hickey to receive the letter. Hickey told Curran that, for the good of the university, he (Hickey) would begin withdrawing Curran's canonical mission. Curran again would fight the decision, including a long court case he would lose. *America, Commonweal,* and the mainstream media all cried foul, but this time it didn't work. When asked about Curran, Pope John Paul II said the following: "Infallible declarations on any subject have been extremely rare in the history of the Church. If you believe only those declarations, you have very little left to believe."

Chapter Five

ASTRAL WEEKS

EARLIER IN THIS BOOK, I DESCRIBED MEETING A woman from India at a dance. We had gotten along well, and at the end of the night I tried to kiss her. She said no, instead kissing me on my cheeks and forehead. It was a new beginning for me, a baptism in the wonderful freedom of self-mastery and restraint.

After that night, that person became a great source of joy for me. She was not familiar with Washington, D.C., my hometown, and we covered the city together. We went to see shows at the Kennedy Center, Mass at the National Shrine, Hindu celebrations, and Nationals baseball games. She introduced me to Indian food and the Bhagavad Gita. We went dancing, talking afterward in the parking lot late into the night. We watched opera on the Jumbotron at Nationals Stadium and saw a taping of the Catholic news show *The World Over* live at the Pope John Paul II Cultural Center. One night we saw jazz singer Kurt Elling, who had electrified me two years earlier with his recitation, during a rendition of "My Foolish Heart," of the poetry of the great sensual mystic Saint John of the Cross. On the night we saw him, Elling performed "Dedicated to You," a sublime tribute to songs first done by Johnny Hartman and John Coltrane.

Later that night my friend and I were at a neighborhood block party, and she overheard me telling someone how we had met. I was about to reveal the way she had first kissed me, but when I saw her face I stopped. I could tell she did not want me to share that part of our lives. Later I asked her if I had gone too far. She smiled and touched my face. "It's OK," she said. "Just remember, the private joys we have shared are special because they belong only to us and to God."

Ironically, the best way to prove the point of this book and practice the difficult but ultimately freeing high adventure of Christian orthodoxy is to not write about my wondrous experience with my Indian friend. To keep it where it belongs, between us and God. But there is nothing to stop me from writing about whom she reminds me of—my favorite saint, Teresa of Avila.

The sixteenth-century Spanish Carmelite and mystic was beautiful, passionate, and brilliant. A friend to Saint John of the Cross, whose work had so inspired John Paul II, Teresa reformed the Carmelite order and developed contemplative prayer as a penetrating and mystical way of achieving union with God. In her work *The Interior Castle,* Teresa envisioned the soul as a castle made out of diamonds, with God at the center. In order to achieve spiritual growth, one had to move through the various "dwelling places" of the castle. It was a journey that required a person to slowly shed his or her own self-interest and self-seeking, surrendering to God; His grace and love then expanded the soul, allowing the seeker to become a radiant, overflowing vessel of sharing God's love.

The journey through the seven dwelling places is filled with eros; as theologian Denys Turner put it, "that eros which is the dynamic of the soul's return to God is one and the same with the erotic outflow from God which is our creation." Of course, in this eros the agape of God, the love that descends from heaven rather than ascends from the earth, is not lost. As Teresian scholar Gillian T. W. Ahlgren notes, "in God, there is an essential unity of all loving activity." In essence, what happens as the soul moves toward God is that eros becomes agape. As we shed our sins and limitations and self-seeking, love breaks out into a dynamic form that seeks outwardly to love others, even at the expense of limiting the self. It becomes, as Pope Benedict XVI once put it, "a love that goes all the way, even to the cross." In *Deus Caritas Est*—God is Love—Pope Benedict XVI's 2005 encyclical, the pontiff gracefully examines how in true love eros becomes agape: "No longer is [love] self-seeking, a sinking into the intoxication of happiness; instead it seeks the good of the beloved: it becomes renunciation, and is ready, and even willing, for sacrifice."

Moving through the interior castle of the soul involves pain, fear, and anxiety. It involves what Pope Benedict XVI elegantly described as the ability to conquer yourself:

> Today an illusion is dangled before us: that a man can find himself without first conquering himself, without the patience of self denial and the labor of self-control; that there is no need to endure the discomfort of upholding tradition, or to continue suffering the tension between the ideal and the actual in our nature. The presentation of this illusion constitutes the real crisis of our times. A man who has been relieved of all tribulation and led off into a never-never land has lost what makes him what he is; [he] has lost himself.

The alternative is liberalism, which has become a religion of resentment. As we have explored, in his 1960 book *Love and Responsibility*, Karol Wojtyla explained the meaning of resentment. Attaining the good requires effort, he wrote—sometimes heroic effort. "So in order to spare ourselves the effort, to excuse our failure to obtain this value, we minimize its significance, deny it the respect which it deserves, even see it as in some way evil, although objectivity requires us to recognize that it is good." Resentment is different from liberal or conservative social activism, which is often the result of a sadness about the state of the world that nonetheless recognizes the reality of the good. In *Love and Responsibility* Wojtyla cites Saint Thomas Aquinas, who defined the cardinal sin of sloth as "a sadness arising from the fact that the good is difficult." But, wrote Wojtyla, "this sadness, far from denying the good, indirectly helps to keep respect for it alive in the soul." Resentment, on the other hand, "devalues that which rightly deserves respect, so that man need not struggle to raise himself to the level of the good."

Our postmodern culture has concluded that the struggle to raise oneself to the objectively good is in itself evil. What is particularly disappointing is the number of Catholic leaders and public figures who have submitted to this new orthodoxy. In 2008, Catholic journalist E. J. Dionne came out in favor of gay marriage after opposing it for most of his life. Dionne, a columnist for the *Washington Post*, made his argument based on conservatism and natural law. Certain conservative thinkers had argued that marriage provides stability and that allowing gays to marry would thus make society more stable. Quoting liberal journalist Jonathan Rauch, Dionne argued that homosexuality was natural—that there had always been and always would be gay people. The natural law, which Catholics believe is revealed to human beings through observation of the world and human reason, shows that homosexuality is just a basic part of the world. "As it happens, I am one of the millions of Americans whose minds have changed on this issue," Dionne wrote. "Like many of my fellow citizens, I was sympathetic to granting gay couples the rights of married people but balked at applying the word 'marriage' to their unions."

Thirteen years earlier, Dionne had written against gay marriage: "That word and the idea behind it," he wrote, "carry philosophical and theological meanings that are getting increasingly muddled and could become more so if it were applied even more broadly."

I agree with Dionne—at least up to a point. The record store I worked at in the 1980s was in a part of Washington with a large gay population and many of the people who worked at the store were gay. One man I became friends with, Matthew, told me about the suffering he endured trying to act straight when he was growing up. He forced himself to go to dances with girls in order to gain acceptance from his family and peers. It was a painful and terrifying experience.

Yet human reason and the natural law also reveal another truth: The male and female bodies are different. This basic fact of human biology makes clear why the argument over homosexuality is so explosive and irreconcilable to the truths of natural law. Gay people are born, not made. The male and female bodies are different. Throughout history, cultures have mounted safeguards against sexual practices that were considered dangerous and unhealthy. And yet if homosexuality is natural, is it dangerous and unhealthy? This dilemma has led many people to settle for a compromise: They increasingly accept gay people, yet are reluctant to fully sanction homosexuality with the imprimatur of marriage. Many, like me, Dionne, and former Vice President Dick Cheney, think the states should be allowed to make these decisions for themselves. Yet what is interesting is how, in embracing gay marriage, many Catholics have abandoned the totality of the natural law—and even become hysterical, punishing advocates for liberalization. They have gone from understanding and wanting to reason with traditionalists to refusing even to engage arguments from the other side. This leads to arguments that are repetitive, propagandist, and frequently unmoored from reason and common sense. And in Dionne's case, it didn't have to be this way. He was once one of America's most interesting journalists.

Exploring Dionne's career in some detail reveals that the problem with American Catholicism is not that it has drifted to the right, but that Catholic liberalism has drifted left. Dionne gained his reputation in 1991 with the publication of his book *Why Americans Hate Politics*. In it, he dissected American politics since the 1960s, concluding that Americans hated politics because they were offered "false choices" by both the left and the right. Citizens didn't want people to starve, yet recognized that large welfare payments could make people lazy. They wanted abortion to be legal, but with restrictions. Vietnam made them doubt foreign wars, but they retained respect for the military. America was a both/and, not an either/or, country. Reread today, *Why Americans Hate Politics* still seems fresh, not least because of Dionne's ability to honestly engage the arguments of conservatives—and to criticize the left. Here he is on the new left of the 1960s:

> Yet as the 1960s went on and the political energies of the New Left focused more and more on cultural issues and the war, the movement began defeating its own purposes. Anger at the American government was transformed into hatred of American society. Avant-garde culture and morality created a gulf between the left and the mass of Americans who favored social reform but lived by a traditional moral code. Thus, when the theory of "participatory democracy" was applied, in an admittedly imperfect way, to the Democratic party, it ended up concentrating power into the hands of a culturally "advanced" upper middle class. This hardly advanced the cause of democ-

racy, since the upper middle class already had much power in both parties.

Dionne then examines the rise of the neoconservatives, liberals who became disenchanted with the excesses of the new left and the counterculture. And to Dionne, they often had good cause to be. "The tragedy for liberals is that they had much to learn from the neoconservatives. . . . In particular, the neoconservatives were right in seeing virtue as a legitimate goal of government policy—even if they were wrong in using virtue as a battering ram against democracy, which they sometimes did." Furthermore, the neoconservatives "were right in insisting that a democratic system depended on citizens capable of exercising discipline and self-restraint—even if their fears about the assaults of the New Left and the counterculture on such values were exaggerated." Dionne then ends the chapter with this hammer blow: "Over time, liberals were no longer certain what kind of family was worth encouraging; they feared welfare programs that required recipients to work; they nearly always saw understandable worries about law and order as covert forms of racism; and they came to believe that almost all doctrines emphasizing the value of local community were indistinguishable from the phony 'states' rights' argument used by segregationists."

This is not to give the impression that Dionne was a conservative. One of the more salient connections he draws in *Why Americans Hate Politics* is between the counterculture of the 1960s, with its calls for no restrictions, and the perils of consumer capitalism. While acknowledging that the government made blunders, he defends the Great Society. But through *Why Americans Hate Politics* his argument remains grounded in reasoned intelligence and common sense—if not what Catholics like Dionne (and myself) call the natural law. It's important to strive to improve society, Dionne concludes, and to use government in a reasonable way toward that end. But human beings are imperfect and utopia not possible. And we know in our hearts what is right and wrong.

In *Why Americans Hate Politics*, Dionne is particularly strong on racial issues. While writing that black rage over centuries of racism was understandable, he defends whites who in the 1960s and '70s were frightened of the pathologies that had taken over the inner cities. In 1988, Republican presidential candidate George H. W. Bush toured flag factories and ran ads pointing out that his opponent, Michael Dukakis, had allowed black criminal Willie Horton out on a furlough, where he killed again. Dukakis criticized the Republican campaign of "flag and furloughs," but Dionne was having none of it: "But 'flags and furloughs' spoke precisely to the doubts that many Americans developed about liberalism from 1968 onward. In the eyes of many of their traditional supporters, liberal Democrats seemed to oppose personal disciplines—of family and tough law enforcement, or community values and patriotism—that average citizens, no less than neoconservative intellectuals, saw as essential to holding a society together." Furthermore, "black separatism . . . encouraged the most subtle kind of racism: the refusal to admit that certain values were color-blind and worth promoting in the ghetto no less than outside."

On abortion, Dionne called for compromise. Most Americans wanted abortion to be legal, but not for the entire nine months. In *Why Americans Hate Politics*, Dionne endorsed restriction on late-term abortions—a stance he would not defend in later years.

Over time, Dionne, like liberalism, lost the wisdom of his former self. He seemed to have become unhinged during the disputed 2000 election, then bedazzled by Barack Obama. After 2000 and then 2008, Dionne grew more and more unreasonable and more dogmatic—not to mention lazy. The difference is clear in the 2004 introduction to the reissue of *Why Americans Hate Politics*. In fact, it's possible to mark Dionne's transformation from level-headed Dr. Jekyll to a milquetoast left-wing Mr. Hyde down to the paragraph. In the introduction, Dionne offers a brisk update of the thirteen years that had elapsed since *Why Americans Hate Politics* was first published. The summary is mostly sound and lucid. Dionne notes that President Clinton balanced the budget even while raising taxes. Crime fell during his presidency. Al Gore endorsed government assistance to religious charities. Most Americans, while disgusted with President Clinton over the Lewinsky scandal, were against impeachment. And so on.

Then comes the 2000 election. And off come the wheels. When the election result was disputed, "the toughness inside the Republican party (and among allied organizations and political commentators) re-emerged." This made things difficult for liberals, because—hold on—"Democrats were slow to come to Gore's defense as he demanded recounts that were perfectly typical of very close elections—and seemed all the more justified in Florida, given the disenfranchisement of so many Democratic voters."

It's like watching a skilled surgeon's hands begin to shake. Suddenly, the Rhodes Scholar and *Post* eminence is churning out "facts" that simply aren't true. Democrats were anything but slow in backing Al Gore and the recounts the former vice president asked for were confined to heavily Democratic precincts. From there, like some horrible journalistic domino theory, Dionne's integrity begins a rapid collapse. He claims that President George W. Bush, the victor in a close election, blew his mandate to govern from the center by cutting taxes for the wealthy. After 9/11, Dionne writes, Bush squandered the opportunity to work with Democrats:

"Bush had opposed the creation of a Department of Homeland Security when Democrats had proposed it after 9/11. But when questions finally arose over what Bush had done (or failed to do) in the pre-9/11 period, he changed the subject by embracing the Democrats' idea." Worse, "Bush accused the Democrats of being insufficiently tough in their approach to the war on terror." And, of course, there's Iraq: "The administration failed to find the weapons of mass destruction it had insisted Saddam held in abundance."

The old E. J. Dionne, the E. J. Dionne of *Why Americans Hate Politics*, would never have written those sentences or been that lazy. Without losing his liberal bona fides, he could have presented the full story: Bush cut taxes, yes—and the economy boomed. He created the Department of Homeland Security not out of some fear of criticism that he had not done enough to prevent 9/11, but because he wanted to protect the country. President Bush never accused the Democrats of being insufficiently tough in the war on terror—although after Senate Majority Leader Harry Reid announced "This war is lost," he would have had cause. Bush criticized Democrats for voting for the war in Iraq—a resolution to use force passed handily in the House and Senate—and then turning against the war when things got tough. Dionne doesn't reveal any of this. The author of *Why Americans Hate Politics* once cited history books, policy journals, newspapers, intellectuals, and regular people, creating a mosaic that was very close to reality. In one part of his book, he quotes a woman in the 1960s who says she is against the Vietnam War—but that the protesters and professors are even worse. These days Dionne won't even admit that most intelligence organizations in the world, not just the United States and Britain, thought Saddam Hussein had weapons of mass destruction.

Just as disappointing is Dionne's weakness on race. In 2008 he fell hard for Barack Obama, giving the future president a pass he never would have offered Stokely Carmichael and other black radicals from the 1960s. In 2008, Dionne delivered a love letter to Obama in the form of an essay in the *New Republic*. Obama's connection to racist preacher Jeremiah Wright had just broken, bringing Obama what Dionne called "the week from hell." Then Dionne offers this: "Obama surely must feel, at the very least, the bitter irony: Few recent presidential candidates have spent more time wrestling with the politics of religion." The old Dionne would not have seen the irony, either—because there is none. Obama entered politics as a young man in urban Chicago, a center for black nationalism. The blowback he eventually got from his friendship with Reverend Wright was the simple result of that. There was nothing ironic about it at all. And the old E. J. Dionne would have seen that. Rather than a soporific mash note, he could have published a compelling examination of the failures of the Black Power movement—and how whites were right to reject it. When Professor Henry Louis "Skip" Gates of Harvard was arrested by a white police officer for being disorderly, causing a national debate, Dionne called for an end to "racial score-settling." The old E. J. would have had the guts to call Professor Gates out on his Black Power resentment. He would have passed a judgment.

A couple years ago, Dionne was on television debating conservative Tucker Carlson. Abortion came up and Dionne argued that most Americans were for keeping it legal. Yes, Carlson said—but with no restrictions? Dionne sat there silently and Carlson pushed: None? he repeated. No restrictions at all? Dionne sat, waiting for the moderator to change the subject. In the journey from journalist to dogmatist, Dionne has become a shrill and predictable writer. He has traded the integrity of the investigative journalist and intellectual for the frisson of the propagandist. This is especially dispiriting because Dionne is a Catholic. What has made writing by Catholics from G. K. Chesterton to Anne Rice so compelling is the tension between reason and political correctness, between the natural law and modernism. The natural law, Catholics believe, is the law that the conscience dictates—the law that tells everyone, regardless of who they are or where they live, that rape and murder are intrinsically evil. According to Saint Ambrose, who is quoted in the Catechism of the Catholic Church, the conscience is "God's herald and messenger," guiding human beings about right and wrong. And while the conscience is a proper guide, Catholics also believe that it needs to be developed; this is done by adhering to the gospels and the teaching of the Church. Catholics further believe that God has revealed Himself through human reason. In Dionne's early writing this tension was evident and made for compelling reading. A good liberal, he was willing to call America on racism, excessive capitalism, and anti-government zealotry. A reasonable man and faithful Catholic, he was equally able to challenge the left on reverse racism, condescension toward working-class whites, sexual promiscuity, and abortion fanaticism. Now he's just another hack.

Many of the new Comstockers tell us that the sex they have is none of our business; yet they seek validation for their beliefs at every turn. One of the most vocal and visible of these is the writer Andrew Sullivan, who is representative of modern liberal Catholicism. Sullivan is a popular blogger who constantly reminds the world that he is gay, that he is Catholic, and that his Church is fundamentally mistaken in its attitude toward sex. He once did this with a great deal of eloquence and fairness. In his 1995 book *Virtually Normal*, Sullivan argued the case for acceptance of homosexuality. He broke opponents of homosexuality into four groups: Prohibitionists, Liberationists, Conservatives, and Liberals. The Prohibitionists believe that homosexuality is "a crime against nature itself," and as such should be discouraged and even prosecuted. Yet, writes Sullivan, "the most depressing and fruitless feature of the current debate about homosexuality is to treat all versions of this argument as the equivalent of bigotry. They are not. In an appeal to 'nature,' the most persuasive form of this argument is rooted in one of the oldest traditions of thought in the West, a tradition that still carries great intuitive sense. It posits a norm—the heterosexual identity—that is undeniably valuable in any society and any culture, that seems to characterize the vast majority of humanity, and without which our civilization would simply evaporate; and it attempts to judge homosexuality by that norm."

In *Virtually Normal*, Sullivan skillfully examines how the Catholic Church's position on homosexuality changed during Vatican II. The 1960s council declared that certain people were predisposed to homosexuality and not to be condemned—only homosexual acts were. He calls for gay marriage and abolishing the ban on gays in the military, yet writes that it must be done with a spirit of goodwill and understanding for those of opposing views. Yet in the years since *Virtually Normal* was published, Sullivan has grown more hectoring, didactic, and hysterical. In his 2006 book *The Conservative Soul* Sullivan argues that anyone who claims that there is such a thing as objective truth is not a conservative, but a fundamentalist. "The essential claim of the fundamentalist is that he knows the truth," he writes. "The fundamentalist doesn't guess or argue or wonder or question. He doesn't have to. He knows." In contrast, writes Sullivan, the true conservative's only guide is his conscience. The conscience is protean, however, and in Sullivan's case, prone to New Age bromides. "As humans, we can merely sense the existence of a higher truth, a greater coherence than ourselves; but we cannot see it face to face," he writes. According to Sullivan,

> We see the world from where we are, and our understanding of the universe is intrinsically rooted in time and place. We can do all we can to increase our knowledge and gain deeper and deeper insight. We can read history and philosophy; we can travel; we can ask questions of young and old; we can debate; we can pray; we can grow through the pain and amusement of daily life. But we will never fully or completely transcend where we are. And even if we could, such transcendence would render us unintelligible to those still earthbound.

Sullivan pits the wisdom of the human conscience against the "diktats" of fundamentalism. He cites an address given in 1991 by Cardinal Joseph Ratzinger, who would become Pope Benedict XVI. In "Conscience and Truth," according to Sullivan, Ratzinger "couldn't have been clearer about how an individual conscience is by no means, for him, the final arbiter of morality or truth." As Sullivan describes it, Ratzinger believes there are two types of conscience. The "self-consciousness of the I" is prone to subjectivity and error. The "deeper conscience" (or anamnesis) is created by God—as Ratzinger puts it, "an original memory of the good and the true (both are identical) has been implanted in us."

Thus, "Even when you think you are taking a principled, intelligent moral stand, if you are in disagreement with the Pope . . . you are not in fact exercising conscience. That's a delusion fostered by evil. You are merely demonstrating sin and guilt. There is no conscience distinct from truth, Ratzinger insisted." And since truth is revealed by the Catholic Church, "all protestations of 'conscience' against Church teachings are just further manifestations of sin." According to Ratzinger, "If truth were left up to the individual conscience, then we would live in moral anarchy, with anyone picking and choosing what to believe."

Yet what Sullivan mocks as nonsense is true. People do indeed seem to have "an original memory of the true and the good" that provides guardrails about right and wrong—the "echo" that John Paul II spoke of in *The Theology of the Body*. Saint Ambrose called the conscience "God's herald and messenger." *Gaudium et Spes*, a document from the Second Vatican Council, declares: "In the depths of his conscience, man detects a law which he does not impose on himself, but which holds him to obedience. Always summoning him to love good and avoid evil. The voice of conscience can, when necessary, speak to his heart more specifically: 'Do this. Shun that.'"

The Magisterium of the Catholic Church does not take the place of the conscience, but rather supports it and helps it know or discover the truth. As John Paul II wrote in his encyclical *The Splendor of Truth*, "Freedom of conscience is never freedom 'from' the truth but always and only freedom 'in' the truth . . . the Magisterium does not bring to the Christian conscience truths which are extraneous to it; rather, it brings to light truths which it ought already to possess, developing them from the starting point of the primordial act of faith." It was exactly that voice of conscience that prompted the admirable actions of several people Sullivan cites as heroes—Socrates, Lincoln, and Thomas More (the saint whose name Sullivan took at confirmation). Indeed, in his talk on "Conscience and Truth," Ratzinger, rather than renouncing the conscience, elevated it even above the papacy, recalling the words of the great nineteenth-century convert Cardinal John Henry Newman, who wrote that if he were asked to give an after-dinner toast, he would drink "to conscience first and the Pope afterwards." Ratzinger makes clear that Newman believed in "a Papacy not put in opposition to the primary of conscience, but based on and guarantees it."

The thing "which establishes the connection between authority and subjectivity is truth." Indeed, Newman converted to Catholicism despite declaring that "no one can have it more unfavorable than I of the present state of Roman Catholics." He converted and spent his life fighting the spread of liberalism in Christianity, because his conscience led him to a defense of the truth.

Of course, it's possible to reject this idea of two levels of conscience that interact with each other. One can live one's life guided strictly by one's active conscience, ignoring the conscience that retains a memory of the true, the beautiful, and the good. This results in what Ratzinger calls "a canonization of subjectivity," which is a good alternate title for Sullivan's philosophy. "It is never wrong to follow the convictions one has arrived at," Ratzinger writes. "In fact, one must do so." What is wrong is coming to such convictions "by having stifled the protest of the anamnesis of being."

When an accurate understanding of Ratzinger's thesis is reached, the problem with Sullivan's thesis is apparent. Sullivan himself is a fundamentalist and the worst kind—reactionary, self-righteous, narcissistic, humorless. He valorizes doubt, but has no doubt in the goodness of gay marriage, for instance. The fundamentalist, posits Sullivan, doesn't need to worry about a crisis of conscience—he simply follows the rules of the Bible or the Church. But "for the non-fundamentalist, life is considerably more fraught." For these, "the exercise of

conscience can be an exacting affair." Beyond the Bible
or the Magisterium in Rome, the non-fundamentalist
"must make an effort to ask himself constantly whether
his thoughts and prayers are rationalizing his own desires rather than seeking the truth itself." This "proper
exercise of conscience is grueling," constantly asking
"whether we are self-deluded or engaging in wishful
thinking; and it is always open to further argument or
revelation." Yet to be always and forevermore open to
further argument or revelation means never having to
settle on anything as the truth—except, of course, the
impossibility of objective truth itself.

Sullivan talks about his "moments of struggle" in his
"long engagement" with the Catholic faith. He had questions about the nature of the Trinity, transubstantiation,
and the Resurrection. His conclusion: "Reaching the
answer yes to these questions—and asking them again
and again and again—is not an easy process." Yet like
the most rabid true believer, Sullivan howls with outrage at the injustice done to him by his Church, which
still insists that to live without limits is to live without
the possibility of real choice and genuine love.

Sullivan, a champion of the supposedly hungry and
expansive mind, can't be bothered to engage honestly
with ideas with which he disagrees. He seems to will-
fully misrepresent the views of Cardinal Ratzinger,
and quotes out of context Catholic theologians Richard
John Neuhaus and George Weigel. Apparently for the

thinking, reading, praying conservative like Sullivan, there's just no time to read things one disagrees with or engage opposing arguments honestly. Liberal Catholics such as Andrew Sullivan, E. J. Dionne, Maureen Dowd, and Chris Mathews were apoplectic when scandals involving the sexual abuse of minors by priests began erupting in the first decade of the twenty-first century. They were right to feel outraged, yet at the same time their anger seemed directed more at the Church itself than at the perpetrators. They never seemed to get around to noting that, according to a study by John Jay College, between 1950 and 1992 about 4 percent of the 110,000 priests active in that period had been accused of sexual misconduct involving children—a much lower percentage than within the general population. In ten years, from 1999 to 2009, the Irish government asked people who had been abused in Catholic institutions from 1914 to 1999 to come forward. The commission assigned to take the report gathered 381 claims—and 35 percent of those were not against priests but against lay staff. In 2009, an audit of sexual abuse by Catholic clerics found six legitimate cases.

That's six too many cases, to be sure. But one wonders where the outrage is about the much more prevalent abuse going on in the public schools. A 2007 AP story by Martha Irvine and Robert Tanner revealed a Neronian level of abuse in America's public schools.

"Students in America's schools are groped," it reads. "They're raped. They're pursued, seduced, and think they're in love." Estimates of how many incidents of sexual assault in public schools have ranged as high as 29,000 a year. The AP found 2,500 incidents of sexual abuse in the public schools over a five-year period— but these were only the cases in which the teacher has his or her credentials revoked. In comparison, there were 4,400 cases of sexual abuse in Catholic schools over fifty years, from 1950 to 2000. That's about 220 a year, which is 220 too many. But it's much lower than the contagion of abuse that has taken over the public schools.

So why aren't Christopher Hitchens and Richard Dawkins, the atheists who want to arrest the pope because of the sex-abuse scandal, at the front door of the National Education Association with a pair of handcuffs? Where is Maureen Dowd's snaky sarcasm, Chris Mathews's spittle, and Andrew Sullivan's rage? Below is an excerpt from the 2007 AP story. Read it, and pretend for a moment that the authors are describing a Catholic school:

> The AP discovered efforts to stop individual offenders but, overall, a deeply entrenched resistance toward recognizing and fighting abuse. It starts in school hallways, where fellow teachers look away or feel powerless to help. School ad-

ministrators make behind-the-scenes deals to avoid lawsuits and other trouble. And in state capitals and Congress, lawmakers shy from tough state punishments or any cohesive national policy for fear of disparaging a vital profession.

If this paragraph were written about the Catholic schools, we would be treated to the usual cavalcade of secular sanctimony. We'd get Ann Curry's pained sorrow as she read the excerpt on the *Today* show. We'd have Maureen Dowd's nursery rhymes about a rope-a-dope-pope or something. We'd have Chris Mathews's sputtering outrage.

These liberals are right that the crimes of the sex-abuse scandal should be brought into the public. And yet, when the public disagrees with them about something like gay marriage, suddenly, everything sexual is a private matter.

For example, in his book *The Christian Meaning of Human Sexuality*, Fr. Paul Quay notes that "in no societies, save those decaying in the last stages of individualism, has marriage been considered a private affair. Everywhere it has been subject to social regulation and control. The private will of two people has never been adequate, by itself, to validate their union, whatever their love for one another." Quay itemized the nuptial symbolism that runs through the Bible, from Genesis to Revelation, and writes that the focus of sex should be God, that "total union with one who is not God is impossible . . . only God can own and take total possession of any person without destroying or degrading that person."

Father Quay is also the author of an essay, "The Disvalue of Ontic Evil," that gets to the heart of the new Comstockery. The essay, which appeared in the journal *Theological Studies*, was a complex rebuttal to the Catholic theologians who had proposed a new concept of evil. Stripped of its academic garnish, the argument of the theologians held that the definition of evil could now include things that limit the fulfillment of our needs and desires. As the priest Louis Janssens wrote: "We call ontic evil any lack of a perfection at which we aim, any lack of fulfillment which frustrates our natural urges and makes us suffer. It is the natural consequence of our limitation." Janssens adds: [A man] has a feeling he is lacking something when he becomes aware of his inability to realize all these different [professional, familial, religious, social] values as much as he pleases. . . . Our body is a means to action. But it is also a handicap which impedes our action. This hindrance may hurt us as an ontic evil."

Father Quay rightly recognized this as a revolutionary change in theology. For while Thomas Aquinas thought that there were evils that had no moral component—pain, sickness, death—he refused to call the simple absence of good an evil. Janssens and the new theologians were doing just that. Continues Father Quay: "Freedom of choice delights in creaturely limitations as the stuff out of which personal growth is made—for what sort of growth can there be without time, space, limitation? Only by free moral choice among limited goods and under the limitations of a material world can human beings serve and worship God." Arguments to the effect that the all-good creator somehow created an ambivalent world that is evil "lead logically toward genuine dualism and collapse of faith in God's absolute goodness."

In pondering Janssens's description of ontic evil, the heart of the new Comstockery is revealed. In the post–sexual revolution world, what was evil was not human sin, but limitation itself. Forgotten is the beautiful insight that an essential component of love is the desire to limit one's own freedom for the sake of the beloved. Resentment becomes an expression of anger— even rage—against those who suggest that, without God, there are boundaries to human possibility, but that those very boundaries offer us the chance to choose the good and, therefore, God.

To many Catholic liberals, any mention of the Church and sex—or just the Church, period—elicits an instantaneous and seething diatribe about sex, homosexuality, and contraception. The tirade is not against any human action as such, but against anyone who dares to talk of limits. Thus in 1989, the gay activist group ACT UP disrupted a Mass being held by New York Cardinal John Joseph O'Connor. The protesters screamed, cried, threw blood. One of them yelled to O'Connor, "You're killing me!" O'Connor opposed the death penalty as well as the U.S. involvement in the war in Nicaragua, and just a few weeks earlier had spoken eloquently about the plight of AIDS victims and the need to provide compassionate care for them. None of that mattered to the activists, however. Simply by upholding the Church's teaching that contraception was not the answer to the AIDS epidemic, O'Connor was "killing" gay men.

For the truth is that sex offers a great paradox: The act itself is praised by poets, musicians (indeed it is the great recurring theme of pop music), and progressive-minded public intellectuals—and they are right to do so. It is an experience like no other. Yet the act itself, the very motion and language of the bodies themselves, reveals a meaning beyond the act. Although sex, contrary to thousands of years of Church teaching, is not primarily about procreation, that is an inseparable part of it. While lovers in the act of lovemaking are lost in the world of the other person, their actions indicate a willingness to become parents. Sex is both exhilarating and dynamic simply as an action of passion and desire, but it is also, as John Paul II said, an icon of the interior life of God, who is love. And love, by its very nature, seeks to spread, to create, to be shared with others.

So to reject contraception is to accept sex for what it is: not simply a way to have kids, nor as a method of pure pleasure, but as a form of prayer that allows for the furthest reaches of self-giving—a giving that does not deny the gift of new life and accepts that lovemaking is an expression of the virtues that make good parents. It is in the very movement and expression of the bodies themselves. Sex is fun. It is exciting. It's athletic. But first and foremost, it is a way to love God—and partake in the life of God. It is a sign of the Trinitarian love of Father, Son, and Holy Spirit.

For more than two thousand years—with some notable exceptions—the Church has gotten this basic truth partially wrong. Yet when it realized the full truth with *The Theology of the Body*, the culture was too far gone to listen. Or perhaps not. Where liberal Catholics are hostile to Church teaching, conservative ones often miss signs of the sacred in the popular culture, which they too readily dismiss as sunken in pagan pseudo-sexuality. In 2005 a remarkable film was released, *The New World*, that tells the story of the initial encounter in Jamestown between settlers and Native Americans. *The New World* was released at the same time as *Brokeback Mountain*, a film championed by Andrew Sullivan, which tells the story of the tragic love between two cowboys. *The New World* is magnificent and transcendent—and almost a shot-for-shot alternative to *Brokeback Mountain*, which is a paean to the superiority and selflessness of gay love.

In *The New World*, the fascination between the English and the Indians turns to love when Captain John Smith, played by Colin Farrell, meets Pocahontas, played by the stunning newcomer Q'orianka Kilcher. Like the two cowboys in *Brokeback*, Smith and Pocahontas meet in the wild and fall in love. Yet the depiction of those loves could not be more different. While *Brokeback Mountain*'s sex scenes are over-the-top graphic, reducing the men—like gay pornography—to nothing more than body parts, *The New World* does not have a single shot of nudity. Pocahontas is lavishly filmed as if she were a messenger from God; director Terrence Malick does not use any false lighting in his films, and the shots of Pocahontas in the wild are breathtaking. We see her shoulders, her face, her hair. She is treated like a queen.

When Smith abandons Pocahontas by faking his own death, she is courted by tobacco farmer John Rolfe, played by Christian Bale. They marry and have a child, and Rolfe takes his bride to England. And it is here that the film truly distinguishes itself from the narcissism that is the core of *Brokeback Mountain*. When Pocahontas learns that Smith is alive, she becomes confused, thinking that she had "married" him at Jamestown. Her husband Rolfe summons Smith, who arrives on horseback. Rolfe then leaves Smith and Pocahontas alone to talk—he loves his wife so much that he wants her to have a clean break with Smith, to make a decision on her own. "You are every bit the man I married, and more," Pocahontas tells her husband. She and Smith talk, Smith trying to explain and apologize for his behavior. Then he departs. As the film comes to a close, Pocahontas is seen playing with her small son on the green lawns of England, then shown on her deathbed (the real Pocahontas actually did die in England shortly after arriving). In a voice-over, her husband explains how she accepted her death, seeing it as fair "as long as the child could live."

Here we have the counter-image to the onanism that is *Brokeback Mountain*. In *The New World*, marriage is shown as difficult—part of a world of limitations—but also as a divine calling that results in real joy—the joy that reaches past oneself to another and to future generations. John Rolfe, unlike the gay cowboys, acts with honor toward his wife—even if it means he may lose her in the end. In *Brokeback*, the heterosexual world is a scene of confinement, a prison cell. In *The New World*, it is the ship full of men arriving on Virginia's shores that is the prison. Indeed, when the movie opens, Captain Smith, guilty of "mutinous sayings," is literally chained to the boat. He emerges from the darkness to find light, a land of abundance, and a new love. Contra *Brokeback*, the fecundity of that love results in children and a future.

And joy. When Pocahontas dies in the film, the next scene shows her running through the English gardens as if born again. Her death has resulted in Life.

This kind of sacred bringing of life out of death, of hope in the face of despair, and the reality of life is at the center of both the Christian faith and of rock 'n' roll. In 2009 I took the Indian woman who had changed my life with three kisses to my face to see Van Morrison, who was touring for the fortieth anniversary of his sacramental album *Astral Weeks*. Watching Morrison, I thought of John Paul II—and the great rock critic Lester Bangs. In 1979 he wrote a piece on *Astral Weeks*. When the album came out in 1968, Bangs wrote, he was deeply depressed, "nerves shredded and ghosts and spiders looming across the mind." Bangs was depressed, it was later revealed, because he had witnessed a rape and done nothing to stop it. Then he writes this: "In the condition I was in, [*Astral Weeks*] assumed at the time the quality of a beacon, a light on the far shores of the murk; what's more, it was proof that there was something left to express artistically besides nihilism and destruction." In *Astral Weeks* "there was a redemptive element in the blackness, ultimate compassion for the suffering of others, and a swath of pure beauty and mystical awe that cut right through the heart of the work." This was a tonic, wrote Bangs, because "the self-destructive undertow that always accompanied the great sixties party had an awful lot of ankles firmly in its maw and was pulling straight down."

In another piece, Bangs made this observation: "There's a new culture shaping up [in 1970], and while it's certainly an improvement on the repressive society now nervously aging, there is a strong element of sickness in our new, amorphous institutions. The cure bears viruses of its own." While Bangs is valorized by aspiring rock critics and fans, most miss what rock writer Brian James once noted—that Bangs's "increasing rejection of nihilism and solipsism, the most important development of his late period, is regrettably lost on his followers."

One song on *Astral Weeks* is "Madame George." It's a song about a transvestite, but there is nothing vulgar about it—it is about the humanity of even the strangest of us. "The beauty, sensitivity, holiness of the song," Bangs writes, "is that there's nothing at all sensationalist, exploitative, or tawdry about it; in a way Van is right when he insists it's not about a drag queen . . . it's about a *person*, like all the best songs, all the greatest literature." Bangs then goes on a magnificent digression about the problem of seeing the miracle of each human life, and how doing so can almost be too much to bear. He writes about people opening S&M clubs, claiming that it is "just another equally valid form of love." That makes Bangs "want to jump out a fifth floor window rather than read about it." But worse, writes Bangs, are "the hurts that go on everywhere every day and are taken so casually by all of us as facts of life." Because if you "accept for even a moment the idea that each human life is as precious and delicate as a snowflake," it will be hard to stop hurting every time you walk out your door and see what goes on in the world.

To me, Bangs is not going overboard, but diving into the deep questions that music of the caliber of Van Morrison demands. Can you imagine such a thing running in any newspaper or magazine today, from the *Village Voice* (which would call the anti-S&M barb intolerant) to the *Times* (ditto) or *Rolling Stone?* It would get tossed because pop music editors are more than willing to fight the corporate power, embrace obscure bands, and celebrate the "rebellion" of punk, but are like the Taliban when it comes to their own orthodoxies. They are terrified of breaking out of the glib, know-it-all style that is the template for pop writing; it could mean the loss of a job. And they know better than to talk religion.

Bangs's emphasis on the personhood of Morrison's Madame George and his description of the degradation of the S&M clubs reminded me of another philosopher. In 1968, the year *Astral Weeks* was released, Karol Wojtyla had written a letter. The future pope wrote:

I devote my very rare free moments to a work that is close to my heart and devoted to the metaphysical sense and mystery of the *person*. It seems to me that the debate today is being played out on that level. The evil of our times consists in the first place in a kind of degradation, indeed a pulverization, of the fundamental uniqueness of each human person. This evil is even more of the metaphysical order than of the moral order. To this disintegration planned at times by atheistic ideologies we must propose, rather than sterile polemics, a kind of "recapitulation" of the inviolable mystery of the person.

They are shockingly similar ideas, right down to the italicizing of the word *person*, coming from the pens of two great writers at the same historical moment. It's time we realize that such similar philosophy can come from both a rock fan and a priest—indeed, that they both are seekers after God.

Acknowledgments

I would like to thank my editors, Trace Murphy and Adam Bellow, for seeing this through.

Bibliography

Allers, Rudolf. *Character Education in Adolescence.* New York: Wagner, 1940.

America. "Birth Control and Public Policy." May 11, 1963.

———. "Point of View." December 22–29, 1962.

Arminjon, Blaise. *The Cantata of Love.* San Francisco: Ignatius Press, 1988.

Ball, William. "The Court and Birth Control." *Commonweal,* July 9, 1965.

Bangs, Lester. *Psychotic Reactions and Carburetor Dung.* New York: Anchor, 1988.

Bayles, Martha. *Hole in Our Soul: The Loss of Beauty and Meaning in American Popular Music.* Chicago: University of Chicago Press, 1996.

Catechism of the Catholic Church. New York: Doubleday, 1994.

Chesterton, G. K. *Orthodoxy.* San Francisco: Ignatius Press, 1995.

————. *The Collected Works of G. K. Chesterton: Plays and Chesterton on Shaw.* San Francisco: Ignatius Press, 1989.

————. "The Moderns Rebel Against Modernism." *New York Times,* May 11, 1930.

Collier, James Lincoln. *Jazz: The American Theme Song.* New York: Oxford University Press, 1995.

Commonweal Confronts the Century: Liberal Convictions, Catholic Tradition. New York: Touchstone, 1999.

Curran, Charles. *Loyal Dissent: Memoir of a Catholic Theologian.* Washington, D.C.: Georgetown University Press, 2006.

————. *The Catholic Moral Tradition Today.* Washington, D.C.: Georgetown University Press, 1999.

Dionne, E. J. *Why Americans Hate Politics.* New York: Simon & Schuster, 2004.

————. "Two Roads to Gay Marriage." *The Washington Post,* May 19, 2008.

Gray, Raymond. "The Younger Set." *America,* October 30, 1926.

Greeley, Andrew. "Like a Catholic: Madonna's Challenge to Her Church." *America,* May 13, 1989.

————. "Family Planning Among American Catholics," *Chicago Studies,* Spring 1963.

Hitchcock, James. *Years of Crisis.* San Francisco: Ignatius Press, 1985.

Hildebrand, Dietrich von. *The Encyclical Humanae Vitae: A Sign of Contradiction.* Quincy, IL: Franciscan Press, 1969.

———. *Purity: The Mystery of Christian Sexuality.* Quincy, IL: Franciscan University Press, 1989.

Johnson, Paul. *Modern Times.* New York: Harper Perennial, 1992.

Jones, E. Michael. *John Cardinal Krol and the Cultural Revolution.* South Bend, IN: Fidelity Press, 1995.

Kelly, George. *The Catholic Youth's Guide to Life and Love.* New York: Random House, 1960.

Kevane, Eugene. "The Significance of the Creed of the People of God." *Social Justice Review.* December 1973.

Kinsey, Alfred. *Sexual Behavior in the Human Male.* Bloomington, IN: Indiana University Press, 1998.

Kirsch, Felix. *Sex Education and Chastity.* New York: Benziger Brothers, 1930.

Lasch, Christopher. *The Culture of Narcissism.* New York: Norton, 1991.

———. *The New Radicalism in America 1889-1962: The Intellectual as Social Type.* New York: Norton, 1997.

Mann, Kenneth. "Has the Church Lost Its Soul?" *Newsweek,* October 4, 1971.

Marcus, Greil. *Mystery Train: Images of America in Rock 'n' Roll Music.* New York: Plume, 2008.

May, William E. *Catholic Sexual Ethics: A Summary, Explanation, and Defense.* Huntington, IN: Our Sunday Visitor, 1998.

Maynard, Theodore. *The Story of American Catholicism.* New York: Doubleday, 1960.

Murphy, Joseph. *Christ Our Joy: The Theological Vision of Pope Benedict XVI.* San Francisco: Ignatius Press, 2008.

Murray, Albert. *Stomping the Blues.* New York: Da Capo Press, 1989.

O'Brien, John. "Let's Take Birth Control Out of Politics," *Look,* October 10, 1961.

Piereson, James. *Camelot and the Cultural Revolution: How the Assassination of John F. Kennedy Shattered American Liberalism.* New York: Encounter Books, 2007.

Pope Benedict XVI. *God Is Love: Deus Caritas Est.* San Francisco: Ignatius Press, 2006.

———. *Jesus of Nazareth.* New York: Doubleday, 2007.

Pope John Paul II. *Love and Responsibility.* San Francisco: Ignatius Press, 1993.

———. *The Splendor of Truth.* Boston: Pauline Books and Media, 1993.

——— and Michael Waldstein. *Male and Female He Created Them: A Theology of the Body.* Boston: Pauline Books and Media, 2006.

Pope Pius XII. *Four Great Encyclicals.* Deus Press, 1961.

Quay, Paul. *The Christian Meaning of Human Sexuality.* San Francisco: Ignatius Press, 1988.

———. "Contraception and Conjugal Love." *Theological Studies* 22 (1961).

————. "The Disvalue of Ontic Evil." *Theological Studies* 46 (1985).

Rock, John. *The Time Has Come.* New York: Knopf, 1963.

Saint Augustine, Bishop of Hippo. *The Confessions of St. Augustine.* New York: Image Books, 1960.

Saint John of the Cross. *The Collected Works of St. John of the Cross.* Washington, D.C.: ICS Publications, 1991.

Saint Teresa of Avila. *Selections from the Interior Castle.* San Francisco: HarperOne, 2004.

Sanger, Margaret. "The Woman Rebel: No Gods No Masters," Margaret Sanger papers, Library of Congress, 1914.

————. "Birth Control Advances: A Reply to the Pope." Margaret Sanger papers, Library of Congress, 1931.

Savage, Dan. "So You've Decided to Break Your Chastity Pledge." *The Stranger,* September 30, 2006.

Scheler, Max. *Ressentiment.* Milwaukee, WI: Marquette University Press, 1994.

Sheen, Fulton. *Old Errors and New Labels.* New York: Alba House, 2007.

Sterns, Marshall W. *The Story of Jazz.* New York: Oxford University Press, 1970.

Sullivan, Andrew. *The Conservative Soul: Fundamentalism, Freedom, and the Future of the Right.* New York: Harper Perennial, 2007.

————. *Virtually Normal: An Argument About Homosexuality.* New York: Vintage, 1996.

Trilling, Lionel. *The Moral Obligation to Be Intelligent.* New York: Farrar, Straus and Giroux, 2000.

Turner, Steve. *Hungry for Heaven: Rock 'n' Roll and the Search for Redemption.* Downers Grove, IL: Intervarsity Press, 1995.

Witham, Larry. *Curran vs. Catholic University: A Study of Authority and Freedom in Conflict.* Washington, D.C.: Edington-Rand, 1991.